Liturgy and Liturgical Formation

Romano Guardini

Translated by Jan Bentz

Nihil Obstat
Deacon Daniel G. Welter, JD
Chancellor
Archdiocese of Chicago
May 31, 2022

Imprimatur
Most Rev. Robert G. Casey
Vicar General
Archdiocese of Chicago
May 31, 2022

The *Nihil Obstat* and *Imprimatur* are declarations that the material is free from doctrinal or moral error, and thus is granted permission to publish in accordance with c. 827. No legal responsibility is assumed by the grant of this permission. No implication is contained herein that those who have granted the *Nihil Obstat* and *Imprimatur* agree with the content, opinions, or statements expressed.

LITURGY AND LITURGICAL FORMATION © 2022 Archdiocese of Chicago: Liturgy Training Publications, 3949 South Racine Avenue, Chicago, IL 60609; 800-933-1800; fax: 800-933-7094; email: orders@ltp.org; website: www.LTP.org. All rights reserved.

Translated by Jan Bentz from *Liturgie und Liturgische Bildung* © 1992 Matthias Grünewald Verlag, Mainz, Germany. The translation was made possible in part by a grant from Adoremus: Society for the Renewal of the Sacred Liturgy.

This book was edited by Kevin Thornton. Michael A. Dodd was the production editor, and Matthew B. Clark was the designer and production artist.

Shutterstock/311472500. Back cover photo, public domain, author unknown (circa 1920).

26 25 24 23 22   1 2 3 4 5

Printed in the United States of America

Library of Congress Control Number: 2022941335

ISBN: 978-1-61671-677-6

LLF

CONTENTS

Foreword to the English Edition   iv

Preface to the English Edition   vi

Translator's Note to the English Edition   xi

Chapter One

The Cultic Act and the Contemporary Task of Liturgical Formation

1

Chapter Two

Liturgical Formation

9

Chapter Three

The Liturgical Mystery

85

Chapter Four

Historical Action and Cultic Event

121

Chapter Five

A Word Regarding the Liturgical Question

133

FOREWORD
TO THE ENGLISH EDITION

In a famous letter written in 1964 on the occasion of the Third Liturgical Congress in Mainz (chapter 1 of this book), Guardini argues that the problems of liturgical reform are not, in the first place, problems of texts and rites, but rather something more fundamental. "If I see correctly," he says, "the typical man of the nineteenth century was no longer capable of the liturgical act, indeed he no longer knew what it was." Guardini is referring to the fundamental shift, which took place over a period of centuries, in the way in which man understood himself. The shift moved (1) from a God-centered view of the world to a man-centered view, (2) from an understanding of man in relation to others to an individualistic concept of man, (3) from a wholistic view of the human person, which integrates reason and intuition, to a great divorce between these two basic ways of knowing. The result is an impoverished view of man. Guardini asks the question: Is this stunted man capable of celebrating the liturgy, capable of the "liturgical act," as he calls it? His liturgical writings explore this question in depth. Yes, man is capable of the "liturgical act" because man is basically a *homo liturgicus*, and the capacity is, in a certain sense, innate. But in order for that capacity to be activated, liturgical formation is necessary. Is that what *Sacrosanctum concilium* had in mind when it stressed the need for the formation (*formatio*) and instruction (*institutio*) of both clergy and laity (cf. SC 14–19)? Perhaps many of the liturgical problems of the postconciliar period can be explained by a superficial formation in liturgical texts and rites, but not the more profound formation that Guardini is talking about. Hence his book on liturgical formation has a timeless quality that makes it just as relevant in the 2020s as it was in the 1920s.

Up until now, only a few of Guardini's writings on the liturgy have been accessible to the English-speaking world. While *The Spirit of the Liturgy* (1918) was translated in 1935, and *Sacred Signs* (1922) in 1956, until now *Liturgical Formation* (*Liturgische Bildung*, 1923) has never been available in English. I enthusiastically welcome the present translation by Jan Bentz, which makes Guardini's work available to a larger public and is, therefore, an important contribution to liturgical scholarship. Liturgy Training Publications of the Archdiocese of Chicago is to be warmly commended for undertaking this project.

The German edition of *Liturgie und Liturgische Bildung* (1992), from which this translation was made, is actually an anthology of texts, written at different times and in different contexts, but always timely. The translation of this edition, therefore, includes the following:

1. The letter of Guardini to the Third Liturgical Congress of Mainz (1964), entitled "The Cultic Act and the Current Tasks of Liturgical Formation"

2. *Liturgical Formation* (1923)

3. *On Liturgical Mystery* (1925)

4. A talk given at the Thirty-Seventh Eucharistic Congress of Munich (1960) entitled "Historical Action and Cultic Event"

5. A letter from Guardini to Bishop Stohr of Mainz (1940) entitled "A Word about the Liturgical Question"

Sacrosanctum concilium was concerned above all with liturgical participation. But formation is necessary in order for that participation to take place at a more profound level. These writings of Romano Guardini, available for the first time in English, can lead us to a deeper understanding of the great task of liturgical formation that still lies before us.

Cassian Folsom, OSB

Founder and prior-emeritus of the Monastery
of San Benedetto in Monte, Norcia, Italy
Associate Professor of Liturgy, Pontifical
Liturgical Institute, Rome

PREFACE
TO THE ENGLISH EDITION

The Second Vatican Council stands in the history of the Church as a moment of remarkable change in how Catholics practiced their faith—and nowhere was this more evident than in the way the Church worshiped. To understand why this is the case, we must understand how the liturgical reform movement, which gained steam in the early part of the twentieth century, so informed the Second Vatican Council's treatment of the liturgy. After the Council, Mass *versus populum*, greater use of the vernacular, and newer and simpler rites would become the most recognizable changes associated with the Second Vatican Council's liturgical reform. Yet, in the minds of the Council Fathers, there was another necessary reform, one more important than changing liturgical externals: the formation (or re-formation) of the laity. As Romano Guardini put it, without the education and formation of the faithful, "the reform of the rite and text will not be of much help" (1964 Letter to Mainz Liturgical Conference; chapter 1 of this book).

Pope Francis echoed Guardini when addressing the 68th National Liturgical Week in Italy on August 24, 2017. Today's liturgical efforts are not about making further ritual changes, about "rethinking the reform," since, as he put it, "the liturgical reform is irreversible." Rather, what is needed is the ongoing formation and education of liturgical participants. He says bluntly: "In truth, we know that the liturgical education of Pastors and faithful is a challenge to be faced ever anew."[1]

Romano Guardini was a key figure in the twentieth century liturgical movement. Guardini's 1918 landmark work on Catholic worship, *The Spirit of the Liturgy*, says Pope Benedict XVI in the introduction to his own book of the same title, "may rightly be said to have inaugurated the Liturgical

---

[1]. Pope Francis, Address to Participants in the 68th Annual Liturgical Week in Italy (August 27, 2017), accessed October 17, 2020, http://www.vatican.va/content/francesco/en/speeches/2017/august/documents/papa-francesco_20170824_settimana-liturgica-nazionale.html.

Movement in Germany. Its contribution was decisive."² The topic of liturgical formation would also feature prominently in Guardini's future writing after *The Spirit of the Liturgy*.

One foundational, if often overlooked, resource on liturgical formation is his brief 1923 book *Liturgische Bildung (Liturgical Formation)*, which was subsequently republished along with additional essays in 1966 (and once again in 1992), with little to no emendations, as *Liturgie und Liturgische Bildung (Liturgy and Liturgical Formation)*—the small but dense book you now have before you—existing until now only in German and Italian.

Still later, continuing to reflect on the importance of the liturgy, Guardini's 1956 edition of *Sacred Signs* refers the reader to his book *Liturgische Bildung* when introducing the place of liturgical signs and personal formation: "The person who makes the signs has been baptized, both soul and body, and therefore [is] able to understand (this was the idea) the signs as sacred symbols and constituent parts of the sacrament and sacramental. Then from the practice of them, which can be gained from these little sketches . . . he could move on to a deeper understating of their meaning and justification."³ Forming the modern man for liturgical action, as described here, could rightly be identified as Guardini's life's work.

Seeing the liturgy's sacramental signs and participating in them with "deeper understanding" was on Guardini's mind even near the end of his life. After witnessing a well-formed and educated group of faithful participate in the liturgy, he notes that "no one looked in the book to find out what the events *meant*, but *read* them with their gazes. . . . Today the problems lie beyond reading and writing, but rather in learning how to gaze lively at something" (1964 Letter to Mainz Liturgical Conference; chapter 1 of this book).

The five chapters that compose this, the first English translation of *Liturgie und Liturgische Bildung (Liturgy and Liturgical Formation)* have this very aim in view—namely, to form and educate today's Catholic to see with understanding, with insight, into the great treasure contained in the sacred liturgy. Some of Guardini's formative themes we encounter—and lessons as necessary to learn today as in Guardini's own time—include

---

2. Joseph Ratzinger, *The Spirit of the Liturgy* (San Francisco: Ignatius Press, 2000), 7.
3. Romano Guardini, *Sacred Signs* (St. Louis: Pio Decimo Press, 1956), introduction.

the actualizing of man's symbolic capacity. "Man," writes Guardini, "is the center of the liturgy as symbol-creator and symbol-receiver. He prays through the unity of body and soul. The movement of his prayer manifests through his ensouled body, and the body expresses the soul" (chapter 2). But when man sees himself not as a living composite of body and soul—either by emphasizing his material bodiliness, or else his spiritual interiority—he thwarts his liturgical capacity, his ability to express spiritual realities through his senses, or to receive the living God by the liturgy's sacramental signs. In other words, if the liturgy is to play an effective role in the life of faith, Guardini insists, man must be understood as the "complete package"—the "total person"—material and spiritual.

Another lesson of liturgical formation treats the corresponding nature of sacramental signs. In the sacramental liturgy, material items such as fire and oil, salt and ashes, bread and wine, "are presented to us so that we may come to sense their essential fullness, especially in the moment when they become signs of the supernatural abundance of the Spirit" (chapter 2). The liturgical celebration is unlike the didactic, mechanistic, and technical activities most engaged in by modern man. The liturgy, rather, employs signs, symbols, and sacraments—it is a work of *art*—to manifest unseen realities. "Liturgical formation must begin here," Guardini says.

In perhaps the most philosophical part of *Liturgy and Liturgical Formation*, Guardini tries to show us just how the sacrament's unseen reality—the Mystery of Jesus Christ and his saving work—can now stand before us today. How, in other words, can a historically bound event become in any real way the substantial and efficacious content of the liturgy and its sacraments, here and now? The liturgy is not, he writes, celebrated after the manner of a passion play, mimicking Christ's past work. Rather, this human action of the divine Christ exists *aeviternally*—that is, in a coexistence of both time and eternity (see chapter 3). In this way, the "*past* of the event stands before the eternity of God; out of eternity, it enters this hour. This is the . . . foundational tenor of the celebration whereupon time is embedded in eternity and the here and now rises into transcendence" (chapter 4).

A fourth task of liturgical formation addresses the place of the individual and the community. Whereas much popular and devotional prayer rests on the felt needs, desires, and likes of the individual who prays them, the liturgy is a corporate and ecclesial action, where individual cells live only in the larger Body of Christ. Guardini writes that the liturgy is an action of "the *Corpus*, the objective entirety. In the liturgical act, the celebrating individual inserts himself into this wholeness, takes up the *circumstances* in his expression of self. That is not easy to do truly and honestly. There is a separating quality which must be here overcome; above all, the isolation of the modern individual" (chapter 1).

Related to this fourth task is another lesson in liturgical formation: the submission of the subjective to the objective. The liturgy is based upon objective truths: God, the Paschal Mystery of Jesus, human nature, the Church. The narrow subjectivity of the individual or smaller community broadens and lives only when enlightened by the larger world of objective truth given by the Church in both what she believes and, reflecting this belief, how she prays as a unified whole. Thus, "instead of expressing every feeling that comes to the surface, only the right and objective feelings that are worthy of being pronounced in the face of God ought to be expressed" in the liturgy (chapter 2).

Liturgy and Liturgical Formation's final chapter, a 1940 letter written by Guardini to the Bishop of Mainz, Albert Stohr, recounts many of the successes and struggles of the early liturgical movement. Some in the movement, Guardini says, were liturgical purists—suffering from "liturgism"—and blind to the needs of the modern worshiper. Others overemphasized an excessively practical approach and risked abandoning the Church's great liturgical tradition. In reaction to these, some fostered a misguided conservatism that, while safeguarding the past, showed reluctance to let the liturgy grow and become a living thing for modern man (see chapter 5). While the challenges of today's liturgical movement may not be identical to those Guardini describes, many will sound familiar—hence his evaluation and response to the movement's self-inflicted shortcomings remain relevant.

Romano Guardini's liturgical insights continued their liturgical influence on the Catholic Church long after his death in 1968. Joseph Ratzinger, for example, penned what may rightly be considered the most popular and influential book on the liturgy since the Second Vatican Council and named it *The Spirit of the Liturgy*, an homage to Guardini's own work of the same name. With clarity and boldness—and with echoes of Guardini's own work—he writes: "True liturgical education cannot consist in learning and experimenting with external activities. Instead, one must be led toward the essential *actio* that makes the liturgy what it is, toward the transforming power of God, who wants, through what happens in the liturgy, to transform us and the world. In this respect, liturgical education today, of both priests and laity, is deficient to a deplorable extent. Much remains to be done here."[4]

May this first-ever English translation of Romano Guardini's *Liturgy and Liturgical Formation* help in some way respond to today's need of ongoing formation in the sacred liturgy. The present project has seen the collaboration of many parties: Adoremus: Society for the Renewal of the Sacred Liturgy; Kevin Thornton and Liturgy Training Publications; Jan Bentz, who translated this difficult text; Father Cassian Folsom, OSB, who encouraged the work and penned the foreword; and Jeremy Priest and Joseph O'Brien for reviewing the text.

"A central theme that the Council Fathers emphasized," said Pope Francis during a Wednesday catechesis on the sacrament of baptism, "was the liturgical formation of the faithful, indispensable for a true renewal . . . : to grow in our understanding of the great gift that God has given us in the [liturgy]."[5] Blessed Romano Guardini, pray for us in this effort!

Christopher Carstens
Director,
Office for Sacred Worship,
La Crosse, WI
Editor and Publisher, *Adoremus Bulletin*

---

4. Ratzinger, *The Spirit of the Liturgy*, 175.

5. Pope Francis, Wednesday Audience (November 8, 2017), accessed October 17, 2020, http://www.vatican.va/content/francesco/en/audiences/2017/documents/papa-francesco_20171108_udienza-generale.html.

TRANSLATOR'S NOTE
TO THE ENGLISH EDITION

The only experience when interpreting a work by Romano Guardini that surpasses the joy of reading his thoughts is the difficulty of rendering them understandable in another language. Guardini's language is as rich, fitting, and proper as it is inventive, creative, and neologistical.

Working on the translation, we were often faced with words that were untranslatable due to their obsoleteness, their equivocalness, or their simple inexistence in common language—even in the German original!

Furthermore, Guardini's rhetoric seems to mirror a pedagogy that desires the reader to wade through each difficult conceptual thesis, not by simplifying terms—at the danger of superficializing the thought and thus "breaking the concept down"—but rather by slowly introducing him to hitherto unknown or unfamiliar concepts in order for him to truly grow in his knowledge and understanding of a certain state of affairs, all the while retaining a dense and specific lexicon that the reader must familiarize himself with while reading the actual text.

Some examples may suffice to illustrate this point:

Bildung in simple German could be rendered as *education*. Yet in this text, the word lends itself to be interpreted according to its root, *bilden*, which means "to form" or even "to imagine" ("Bild" = "image"). From the context, it is clear that Guardini refers to "liturgical education" in its general interpretation, yet also in its full anthropological depth, considering that man is truly "changed" by acquiring knowledge in his understanding of the world. Therefore, the translation of *Bildung* as *formation* seems more fitting here, since "to form" carries a stronger sense than "to educate."

Another example would be the word *ensouled*. The word *durchseelt* literally means something that is "fulfilled" or "imbued" with a soul. We found the slightly awkward *ensouled* to be the shortest and most suitable rendering of *durchseelt* in English, since it truly captures the "condition of being imbued with, and completely inundated by, a soul" of a material body.

Equally difficult are technical terms that were more widespread at the time of Guardini's writing. Terms like *Gestalt* and *profan* echo in the early twentieth century respectively as "Gestalt-theory" in psychology, which taught that there was a certain structuralism dominant in the human psyche, as well as Mircea Eliade's distinction of "sacred" and "profane" which certainly implies the—more familiar to a modern reader—term *secular* but with more precise nuances within the philosophy of religion. Here again, we decided to stick with the more technical term rather than sacrifice Guardini's multilayered deliberation for the sake of a simpler word.

In the translation we chose to carefully replace certain antiquated words (that were antiquated even in the original text), while keeping some of the more difficult and technical terms in their English equivalent. This approach seems to us to follow most faithfully Guardini's own way of writing philosophy.

Ultimately, we hope to make this collection of beautiful texts of Guardini accessible to a wide audience who will profit from his rich understanding of reality, the human being, his condition in the world, the Church, and the liturgy.

Jan Bentz, Dr. Phil
Blackfriars Hall, Oxford University

CHAPTER ONE

The Cultic Act and the Contemporary Task of Liturgical Formation

A Letter[1]

Dear friend,

 I had very much wanted to take part in the third liturgical congress in Mainz. On that occasion, I would have been pleased for the opportunity to point something out to you that seems important to me. Unfortunately, that is not possible now; therefore, I will have to be content expressing my thoughts in a letter to you, which I hope will reach its destination.

 Liturgical work—as we all know—has reached a crucial moment. The Council has laid down the basis for the future; how the Council came together and has proclaimed the Truth [of Christ] will forever remain a prominent example of the working of the Holy Spirit in the Church. The question remains where the work needs to begin, so that this recognized Truth can become reality.

 Clearly, a plethora of ritual and textual questions will become urgent, and just how much can be done right or wrong is exemplified by long experience. In my opinion, the main point here seems to be something else:

---

1. The letter was written on the occasion of the Third Liturgical Congress in Mainz, 1964. In the later 1966 German edition of *Liturgie und Liturgische Bildung*, the exact wording was improved by more precise and developed language.

that is, the question of the cultic act or, to be more precise, the liturgical act. If I am not mistaken, the typical nineteenth-century man was not able to perform that act; indeed he was completely unaware of it. For him, religious activity was of an individual and interior character, and when religious activity turned into *liturgy*, this character became the character of official public celebrations. The sense of the liturgical action was lost because what the faithful carried out was not truly a liturgical act, but rather a ceremonial, private, and internal act, which was frequently accompanied by the feeling of a disturbance of the liturgical act. In that context, the efforts of those concerned with the liturgy must have seemed like the peculiarities of aesthetes which were lacking Christian seriousness.

The intensity of the exchange during the Council renewed in the consciousness of those who think in line with the Church that something essential is at stake. Anyone who did not get caught up with secondary things—such as the Church-political significance of the use of the vernacular language—came into the consideration of what this "liturgical act" could be, which everyone was eager to preserve. And anyone who did not get caught up with secondary issues had to come to the conclusion that the liturgical act as a religious event was something significant and important.

Those who set out to seek the essence of what is proper must have come to the conclusion that the liturgical act is carried out by the individual together in a sociological whole, in a "Corpus"—the community, that is, the Church present in it. This act does not just consist of spiritual interiority, but preeminently signifies man as a whole, spirit and body. Therefore, the external action should be itself a "prayer," a religious act. Elements of this action, time, and place are not just external "ornaments" but elements of the action as a whole and must be realized as such with all that it entails.

The usual discussion brings the sociological-ethnological component to the fore: participation of the community and the use of the vernacular language. In truth, much more is at stake: the revival of an action of the whole, a whole world of acts, which has withered and which has to live anew. These considerations have to be recognized first as essential—and there looms a real danger that everything that has been said will be brushed off as an "artificial affectation," especially by those whose inclinations tend toward the individualistic, rationalistic, and external. It must be seen too that this external inclination is not so old indeed, but contemporary, and has in fact repressed the truly old essentials of the Church.

What is being discussed is thus the question of whether this marvelously opened liturgical possibility can be realized to the fullest extent. Maybe it will be exhausted by removing aberrations or will be satisfied by creating something new, by giving better instructions about what acts and things mean, or by the renewed opportunity to learn a forgotten act and retain long forgotten attitudes.

Naturally, the inquiry will appear if the current liturgy has elements that cannot be properly realized by modern man. I recall a discussion with the great—now deceased—pioneer of the liturgical renewal, Abbot Ildefons Herwegen of Maria Laach. After a few preceding remarks, I explained that one of the signs that the liturgical work had been revived would be a *liturgical crisis*, and Abbot Herwegen had to assent pensively. As long as liturgical acts are only objectively *celebrated*, the texts only got through by reading, then everything will go well, since nothing enters the realm of the true religious act. At the moment the action reaches the seriousness of prayer, what surfaces are the parts (of the celebration) that lack living appeal. Those who are endowed with the task of education then have to ask themselves—and this will be most decisive—if they are willing to realize the liturgical act themselves. To express it more clearly: do the educators really know that the act exists, what makes it up, and that they understand that it is neither a "luxury" nor a curiosity, but something essentially constitutive? If what they understand does amount to the same liturgical act, then we end up with a repetition of the error of that pastor from the end of the nineteenth century when he said, "We must organize processions better; we have to care that prayer and singing improves," but forgot that the true question should have been: "How does walking itself become a religious act, an escort for the Lord, Who passes through this land, where a true 'Epiphany' can happen?"

The central question is, What is the constitutive liturgical act? And indeed we can only bring up some indications of the answer at this point.

The essential element of this act is most evident when it becomes a way of acting, for example in the sacrificial walk. There is a specific difference if the faithful only understand this walk as a movement to reach a certain end that could be equally fulfilled by an usher who walks around with the collection basket, and if they know that bringing up the gifts itself is *prayer*, a disposition toward God, a co-realization of the presentation of the gifts. A thing can also be infused with this act of doing, such as the coin as a representation of concrete gifts or the oblation by the priest, the blessing of bread and wine. Then the *meaning* is not said or done in addition to the act, but is realized in the act itself. The same is true for spaces and places within spaces, for times and days and hours.[2]

The liturgical act is realized in *watching*. This does not just entail perception by the sense of sight of what happens at the altar or the recognition of text being read in a book, but is in itself a living participation. I experienced this in the cathedral of Palermo when I felt the full attention with which the people followed the liturgy of Holy Saturday without a book or any other *explanatory* word. Probably much of their attention was just an external *gazing*, but essentially there was more. The gaze of the people was itself an act, in itself a participation in the sacred event.

Only from this point of view can a liturgical-symbolic event be essentially understood, like the washing of the hands of the celebrant or the simple liturgical gesture of the spreading of the hands over the chalice—not in the explanation (this means this and that) but in the symbolic action, whereby the realization of the liturgical act is *done* and is *read* in equal manner by the beholding person in an analogous act; the inner sense is understood by seeing what is external. Otherwise, everything is just a loss of time and energy, and it would be better simply to *tell* the community what is meant. But the symbol in itself is something corporeal and spiritual, an expression of something interior by the external, and must therefore—in order for it to unfold its full potential—be enacted with gravity and recollection[3] and must be participated in by the beholding of the action. There is special importance for the liturgical act in the

---

2. Translator's note: Guardini seems in this gratuitously convoluted expression to mean that the meaning will be imbued in space (general), places within that space (particular), and all moments of time, using the Kantian pure categories: space and time.

3. (The German-language publisher Matthias Grünewald Verlag [hereafter, MGV note] added notes to the 1992 edition of *Liturgie und Liturgische Bildung*. Most are included in this edition.)
MGV note: This poses a difficult problem for liturgical formation: the ability to see and to participate has obviously—in spite of, or perhaps because of, the flood of "images" in modern life—largely disappeared, and it is very much a question of whether it can be recovered. Under these circumstances, shouldn't the word and its reception receive new meaning in cultic action? However, here everything is only in its beginning stage: Do we have a translation of Sacred Scripture at our disposal which can meet the requirements of the cult?

participation of the community. The immediate basis for this seems to be the individual faithful, not as an isolated individual, but as the chain of a *community* in which the Church becomes realized. This community is the subject that speaks the "we" of prayer texts. Its structure is of another kind compared to those which form in any other meeting or for any other purpose. It is the *Corpus*, the objective entirety. In the liturgical act, the celebrating individual inserts himself into this wholeness, takes up the *circumstances* in his expression of self.

Many separating factors must be overcome: most of all the isolation of the modern individual, but also all things that cause aversion and repugnance toward the neighbor—indifference toward the many who do not seem to *concern me*, but who are, in truth, members of my community. Similarly all indolent remaining-in-oneself and so forth.[4]

If the intention of the Council is to be realized, then there is need not only for a correct explanation and true education, but also practice, by which this act may be adopted. The active presence of the people in Palermo rested on the fact that no one looked in the book to find out what the events *meant*, but *read* them with their gazes—surely an aftermath of old-fashioned education and probably paid for by the shortcomings of what is taught in modern primary school. Today the problems lie beyond reading and writing, but rather in learning how to gaze lively at something.

Herein lies—as it appears to me—the actual task of liturgical formation. If this is not understood, then the reform of the rite and text will not be of much help. Yes, it may even happen that the serious people—those who have true piety at heart—will have the feeling that something unfortunate is happening, just as an honorable old parish priest once told me when he said: "Before the liturgical renewal the people were able to pray. Now there is only talking and walking around." It will cost much thought and experimentation in order to bring modern man to truly live the act without turning it into theater and empty gestures. It is not to be forgotten that some of those who should be teachers and leaders are themselves unexperienced in this, or resist it from an individualistic attitude of piety, or feel the duty as an unreasonable imposition and think that this "trend" needs to pass and that "everything will remain the same."

---

4. [Do we understand what speaking and hearing are, which renders the cultic word fruitful?]

The liturgical renewal has undergone many phases. It would be useful and enlightening not just to explain them in historic sequence, but also to retrace their history's internal sense. If a very short summary is permitted, then I want to call the first phase, initiated in Solesmes, the restorative—in some sense even the Church-political restorative. (It was connected with the intent of overcoming Gallicanism and sought a deeper rooting in Rome.) The second originated in Benedictine abbeys and was of a very academic type, leading the faithful immediately back to the texts. The third phase, centered in Klosterneuburg and the Catholic youth movement and youth work, was of a practical nature, always with quick, visible results in mind. It sought community in its daily experience and therefore rendered specific importance to the vernacular language.[5]

Now, based on the impulses of the Second Vatican Council, a fourth phase must begin, a phase that addresses living participation and asks about the nature of the true liturgical event: how is it different from other religion events and how is it different from the freely formed community event that is the "devotional meeting"? What is its foundational act? What is its form? Which errors threaten it? How do its demands relate to the structure and living consciousness of today's people? What has to happen so that today's man can learn it in a genuine and reasonable way?

There are problems and tasks enough—even if one did not have to start with questions for clarification. Is, perhaps, the liturgical act and with it all that is generally called *liturgy* historically bound indeed, ancient or medieval, such that we would have to discard it wholesale anyway? Should we all concede to the realization that the person of the industrial age, the technological age, with his psychological-sociological structures is simply not capable of the liturgical act?

And should we, instead of speaking of renewal, rather not think about the way in which the sacred mysteries are to be celebrated so that the modern person with his perceptions can truly appreciate them?

---

5. MGV note: Perhaps one can add here: With the discovery of the liturgy and its meaning for the community, the liturgy was discovered and realized as an act of the whole Church. One of the most active centers of liturgical renewal, Burg Rothenfels, never understood itself as an "esoteric conventicle," but rather always as a "community"—albeit a community of a special kind: as a congregation in which theological and cultural knowledge and experiences were gained that later (think of the celebration of Holy Week and Easter night) have become fruitful for the whole Church. So one can say that without this knowledge and experience the work of the official institutions would hardly have been possible.

It seems harsh to speak like this. But there are not a few who go all out and think this way. We cannot ignore their plea as though it comes from some *outsiders*, but we have to ask ourselves how we—if the liturgy is truly essential—can approach them.[6]

In truth, there are some very encouraging developments too. It is not accidental that the youngest phase of the Liturgical Movement happened at almost the same time as the awakening of the ecclesiastical sense.[7] The pedagogical movements also simultaneously sprung up, with the intention of bringing forth a true image of man, as that creature in whom body and soul, external and internal, form a true unity, and other such features. From these coincidences the work of liturgical renewal could learn some things. Very serious educators have pointed out that true formation is not exhausted by mere saying, rational explaining, and formal organizing. The sense of vision, of action, of forming must be awakened and become part of the formative event. We have to recognize that the musical moment is more than ornament; that the community means more than merely sitting next to another, indeed it is rather solidarity in living and existing together, and so forth.

Much needs to be said here; I must close now, otherwise my letter will become an epistle. Either way, I am sending my most sincere and heartfelt wishes for the work of the congress.

Yours,
Romano Guardini

---

6. MGV note: In the meantime, the monks of Maria Laach have taken up Romano Guardini's question and made it the subject of a "survey" among lay people, priests, and religious. The result of the survey was just introduced with a significant introduction by P. Burkhard Neunhäuser, osb, under the title "Is Man Still Liturgical Today?" published by *Ars liturgica*, Maria Laach.

7. MGV note: This is the reason why J. A. Jungmann, sj, could write in the commemorative volume for Karl Rahner ("God in World," II, p. 243): "We experience in our century the regeneration of the idea of Church and the cult. The phrase 'The Church awakens in the soul,' with which Guardini opened an essay in *Hochland* in 1922, has been repeated and affirmed repeatedly. Guardini saw this awakening prepared in a new sense for people and a community of people, as he witnessed it in the blossoming Youth Movement of the '20s. But its proper realization he recognized in the awakening of the Liturgical Renewal. The Liturgical Renewal with all that goes along was only possible with the prerequisite of a concept of Church that was filled anew with the old meaning."

CHAPTER TWO

Liturgical Formation

FIRST ATTEMPTS

The essay[1] "Liturgical Education" was published for the first time in 1923. Forty years of intensive liturgical thinking and working have passed. The "Liturgical movement," initially characterized as a "renewal movement," was originally tolerated by prominently ranking circles, eventually supported by the Church's hierarchy, and subsequently entered the movement for reform of the Second Vatican Council, where now it bears fruit for the global Church.

At the Third Liturgical Congress of 1964, held in Mainz, general questions about the basis of and preconditions for liturgical education arose. This sort of education requires a certain groundwork and educational tasks which I have already mapped out in an essay called "The Liturgical Experience and Epiphany"[2] given at the Second Liturgical Congress, held in Frankfurt. I reiterated this a second time in a *letter*, which I penned on the occasion of the Congress in Mainz and sent to the General Secretary of the Liturgical Institute in Trier.[3]

The decisions in support of the reform of the Council triggered a new effort to deal with all liturgical problems in education. This led to the idea

---

1. Pages 1–4 of this chapter (First Attempts), written in 1966, function as a "preface" or "author's note" to Romano Guardini's 1923 essay.

2. MGV note: This essay was published in *Die Sinne und die religiöse Erkenntnis* [The Senses and Religious Cognition], (Würzburg 1958), 36ff.

3. MGV note: First published in: *Liturgisches Jahrbuch*, 2/1964. Due to its significance for the questions mentioned in this present work, it was included in this edition; see chapter 1.

of making an out-of-print book by the title "Liturgical Education—Attempts" accessible and to reprint it.

The initiative met substantial challenges. The work was published in the early 1920s. It rests on the experiences of the younger generation of the time, and targets those of the so-called *Youth Movement* as its audience, appealing to their concepts in language. Consequently, it exemplifies in character the lively, peculiar, and also partially exaggerated time (as is proper for any existential initiation). Therefore, it could not be reprinted without changes—though that would have been easier—for it would have lacked a certain expediency, and it could have damaged the very task that it set out to address.

The publisher and I have therefore decided to rework the book for the current aim, to cut out everything dated, and to integrate to a further extent insights from that time to the modern understanding. The substance of the book, in its reality and validity, was to be made fruitful for the present time [c. 1966]. This created an obstacle of a conceptual and linguistic nature, which was not easy to overcome: the task of giving justice to a past *phase* of liturgical thought and work, as well as to address modern challenges. How much this has been successful must rest with the judgment of the reader.

The first encounter with the liturgy I made was during the time of my studies in Tübingen. It happened between 1906 and 1908 in the Archabbey of Beuron (on the Danube). Personalities such as Rev. Odilo Wolf and others each gave the movement his own personal touch. Back then Beuron was not taken up by so many visitors and pilgrimages. Therefore I could—together with my hence deceased friend Karl Neundörfer, who had studied theology after jurisprudence—live in the monastery. The astonishing impressions made upon me there formed me throughout my whole life. They became ever more profound in connection with the experience of liturgy, the recognition of what the Church is, and the further realization that Christian evangelization is efficacious if it—without making cuts and adaptations—speaks out its sacred message.

In those days, my friend and I made a plan to reveal the essence of the Church through two texts. Perhaps the reader will hear von Ihering's classic work, *Of the Spirit of Roman Law*, resonate in the title of Karl Neundörfer's projected book, *Of the Spirit of Canon Law*, and of mine, *Of the Spirit of the Liturgy*. But plans of that sort have their own fate. My friend met his death in the mountains of Sils-Maria before he could set his hand to such a text. I was given the chance to write the humble work *The Spirit of the*

Liturgy, which the Most Reverend Abbot of Maria Laach, Rev. Dr. Ildefons Herwegen, OSB, published following the urgings of my deceased friend, Dom Cunibert Mohlberg, OSB, as the first book in the series *Ecclesia orans*.

The Spirit of the Liturgy has found wide distribution.[4] And of today, more than forty years later, I can still feel, with some uneasiness, a little too enthusiastic tone of the writing—which was evidently an expression of the joy of discovery—I may equally hope that it fulfilled its task. At the same time, I can only hope that out of the current phase of the *liturgical movement* new work will arise which will explain what the liturgy is; work level with the current understanding as well as the depth of religious life.

As noted, more than forty years have passed since its first publication. Which path has been walked, how much success has been reaped, and how much more *natural* everything has become—a small recollection may make manifest. Not long before the First World War, I told a co-student friend: "I want to have the experience that during a parish Mass, not sung just spoken, I turn to the people and say, 'Dominus vobiscum,' and not just the altar servers but the whole community answers: 'et cum spiritu tuo.'" That was the past. Then the charismatic event of the pontificate of John XXIII came upon us as well as the Second Vatican Council, whose significance—despite much else—seems to lay in the fact that it stands at a moment of the breakthrough of the postmodern world and whose impulses are expressed in its problems as well as in its possibilities.

Much, if not all, that is dependent upon liturgical work must be ascribed to the right place and at the right depth. The re-elaboration of the texts and the explanation of the liturgical elements do not alone conclude the task. Formation concerning what the sacred actions *mean* is also not the most essential element. The time is upon us when we must realize wherein the essence of the liturgical event lies and how it is realized in the liturgical act. We must understand what poses a challenge to the people—men, women, and children—of our time and what has become incomprehensible; further, how they may be touched by experience and through the insights of modern pedagogical and anthropological works.

In this context, the present text is written. It is my wish that the editing that it underwent should bear fruit for this aim.

— **Romano Guardini**

---

4. MGV note: the 25th printing of *The Spirit of the Liturgy* was published in the year 1962.

Introduction

This chapter aims to elaborate what *The Spirit of the Liturgy*[5] has initiated. Shall it enjoy success in this endeavor, it will announce even more clearly what the essence of liturgical life is than did the previous text. Indeed, it will speak out of the deep consciousness of the current time. The text must do so if it wants to successfully establish the prerequisites for a living education. We need not only endeavor into what has always been true, but we must also ask for what is alive in our own time. Perhaps it is even tied to a certain moment of development that is connected to this time. What is decided today will have far-reaching consequences. New powers awaken, new attitudes are formed, even if they only yet linger and remain unnamed. Much will depend upon which name will be written into them. These new *attempts* shall help so that the name may be Jesus Christ. This will mean too that this text is not something that is already set, possessed, and transmitted, but instead it is an attempt comparable to an intuition and a premonition. Within a few years, what remains confused at this time shall be seen much more clearly. Some judgments will prove to be wrong; some expectations will not meet their goals. This text therefore should be seen in the context of being written today (1923!) and not in the years to come.

What is presented here is the first part of these *attempts*. A second will follow.[6] The latter will deal with *liturgical mystery* and other questions that are related to this. The epilogue of this present work, "A Word Regarding the Liturgical Question," will form the closing chapter—even though it should be placed after each chapter—since only through it as a lens will the thoughts expressed gain their proper understanding. Hence

---

5. Abbot Ildefons Herwegen, OSB, *Ecclesia orans* (Freiburg, 1st ed., 1917; 25th ed. 1964). [Editor's note: This was Guardini's own note; however, for clarification, *Vom Geist der Liturgie (The Spirit of the Liturgy)* was first published in 1918 as the first volume of the influential *Ecclesia orans* series editied by Abbot Ildefons Herwegen of Maria Laach.]

6. MGV note: These attempts were continued—[Romano Guardini] loved referring to his works in this way, not because of coquetry, but due to conviction—in his essay, "On the Liturgical Mystery," published in: *Die Schildgenossen*, 5, 1924/25: 285–414—chapter 3 of this book. He took up the theme once more in the book *Meditations before Mass* (Notre Dame, IN: Ave Maria Press, 2014). In *The Essence of the Commemoration of Our Lord,* 8th ed. (Mainz: 1965). [This] book can be considered the guideline of liturgical formation and its significance for the work of reformatory decisions of the Second Vatican Council—its educational work it cannot be underestimated.

it seems right that it should be placed at the end of this book so that out of this midst it shall give everything "measure, number, and weight."

THE TASK

Liturgy does not deal with knowledge, but with reality. There is knowledge of the liturgical action, which precedes it and could be called liturgical knowledge [*Liturgik* in the original German].[7] And there is knowledge within it; the liturgical event allows an insight into itself. To speak about this today is not easy because it has escaped our religious consciousness at large. The liturgy itself is not merely knowledge but a full reality, which embraces much more than knowledge alone: a doing, an order, and the being of itself.

Thus, when we ask ourselves which tasks are assigned to the liturgy, we are not dealing with a scientific endeavor, which would be liturgy (*Liturgik*). We are not dealing with spiritual counseling and magisterium, but mainly with formation, the word taken in its essential meaning. In this way, it wants to lead the individual in his entirety to the religious-cultic behavior, which makes up the essence of the liturgical life.

This task does not impose itself. Liturgy is not a hobby of an elect group of kindred spirits, but it is the center core of the unbroken Catholic-ecclesiastical life itself, neither artificially *made* by the liturgical movement nor simply sprung forth from the awakening will of the fully Catholic-Christian way of life. This fact is unquestionable. Rather, we are dealing with how a truly liturgical life was able to develop. Not just in places where it could flourish due to favorable circumstances, with people who had a special disposition for it, or in the spiritual environment of a Benedictine abbey, but in the everyday life of a parish community. Yet exactly here lies a danger. Whosoever lives the liturgy will be happy about an attempt to unlock its treasures. However, faced with some texts on the liturgy, one will have to admit that only what comes out of its core and essence can truly serve the liturgy in the end.

---

7. Translator's note: There is no proper translation for "Liturgik" in English that is distinct enough to make this logical. In German it is *Liturgie* (that which is liturgically enacted) and *Liturgik* (that which deals with all things liturgical).

If richer knowledge about liturgical things is to be taught and joy awakened regarding liturgical actions, and if liturgical concepts are to become religious exercises even to those who had been strangers to them previously, the result will be a partial success, even if there will always be room for improvement. The central question remains: What is the essence of a liturgical attitude?[8] What would be required of man and the community to be rooted in the liturgy? Which forces and sensitivities need to be activated—even, yes, the core of every person—[that is, his or her being]? We are dealing with a very special skill, a becoming, and a growing; indeed, we are dealing with a kind of being. That means we are dealing with a problem of "formation" in the truest sense of the word.

The forces that presuppose such a skill, the sensitivities from which these forces arise, the whole being that carries these sensitivities—these all have withered since the beginning of modernity. Certainly, one will bring up the objection that this kind of approach ties liturgical action to a specific time and cultural-psychological predispositions. Such an approach is not permitted when dealing with Catholic religious practices—that is, practices true for all times and all levels of culture.

Now it is true that the liturgical life does in a certain way transcend these predispositions. Everyone can participate in the Eucharist and receive the sacraments, including he who is subjectivistic and individualistic. Moreover, recent centuries have brought to light forces which unfolded have promoted the wellbeing of the liturgical life, such as a greater sensibility of the soul, a stronger consciousness of personal subsistence, and the dignity and responsibility, etc., of each. We can find a deeper understanding of the essence, form, and spirit of the liturgy and no one will doubt that this rests on a "formation" which since the Middle Ages has slowly waned into disappearance. What remains in question is: Is this kind of formation tied to a specific time such that it will vanish once the frame of that time has vanished definitively? Or are we dealing with the universal human potentiality of the human essence and powers that always reawaken as soon as the conditions for their awakening are given anew? It is this latter conviction upon which this text rests. Delving deeper it becomes even clearer: those things that make the future, what we sense in the coming of

---

8. See Romano Guardini, *Meditations before Mass*, part 1; see note 5 above.

a future age, are to a certain degree forces of this kind. They seek life at the surface; they seek to regain long lost attitudes and to unfold withered sensitivities. A new striving for formation ferments interiorly in a renewed movement toward life and the revived will for one's own formation. Deficient in proper sensitivities, forces, and attitudes, our Catholic life languished, thin and rationalistic; yet now, these very elements are reawakening. We certainly do not want to return to the Middle Ages; we want our own present and future. Yet we yearn for those forces by which the Middle Ages were so mighty in imagery; we long for them to awaken again in our time and for the boon of our contemporaries. Despite the destruction of the past, we can trust that there is truly something coming to life anew.

Among those powers we have mentioned are those that need to be alive in order to render liturgical life real. By a movement of inner necessity, our time is ripe for the liturgy. Moreover, among the final challenges we face is to discern whether this new life that is surfacing can be elevated into liturgy and so participate in the formation of "all under one head, Christ" (Eph 4:15). Or will liturgical formation remain merely a formation of culture, a certain power of expression of man, man's being in the world, and his natural feelings of devotion? Therefore, the liturgical problem, seen in the right context, will be one of the most pressing spiritual and cultural issues of the future.

Each chapter of this book contemplates the liturgical life under one specific aspect. Together they ask: What becomes of liturgical method? Is enough importance given to it in our time; and if not, then why not? Which forces lack in man to renew the liturgy, and will these forces reawaken?[9] The concrete tasks of formation in the liturgy will emerge in all clarity out of these explanations.

Considering all of this, we need to focus on the essentials. We can only deal with what needs to be done in individual cases to the extent that we may emphasize certain basic and fundamental thoughts. How either the child or the mature person can be led to liturgical action, or even how this can be done with a community, is an inquiry that will need to be left for others to explain. The path only reveals itself once one endeavors to treat it. But to show that we are not just playing around with thoughts,

---

9. It is natural that the youth movement together with its impulses, forces, and goals be mentioned frequently in these considerations. In a broad sense, it implies the emergence of a certain image of humanity, which embodies the turning point for a new future.

our passages will be completed with some practical advice. This does not mean that there is a prefigured method, but these are supposed to help to initiate the process of resolution.

SOUL AND BODY

The center of the liturgical action, the one who prays, sacrifices, and acts, is not the *soul*, not even *interiority*, but it is the *person*. The whole person carries liturgical action. The soul is certainly crucial, but insofar as she ensouls the body. Interiority, to be sure is as well, but only as far as it is revealed through the body—*anima forma corporis*. This sentence of the Council of Vienna (1311–1312) reveals its whole meaning thus: our soul is a spiritual substance, which is independent of the body in its being, but essentially determined to be the forming, life-inducing, and action-enabling principle of the body. We must see this truth for all its clarity. In every theory of dualism, the body does not pertain to the dignity or the essence of man, it is only regarded as something trivial, lowly, or even evil. The soul, according to this logic, becomes *imprisoned* in the body and assumes the task of freeing herself from it. This is the thought of Neo-Platonism, Gnosticism, Manichaeism, and some currents of modern thought. Simply put, it is puritanism. Puritans all want *one* soul, a *spiritual*, purely *internal* devotion, and they think everything bodily is a depressing contamination. Pietism replaces bitter spirituality with the inner fulfillment of the soul. But its religion of interiority is at best something dualistic. Even here, the body is not accepted as part of the subject, which carries the religious action and attitude. All of these schools of thought tear apart the essential unity of the soul and body, or at least loosen it. Thus, they lack something essentially human. In stark contrast stands monism, which postulates that the two are only one: body and soul are just two sides of the same living unity. The body is a *thickening* of the soul; the soul is the *inner side* of the body, indeed something *of the body*. Here, religion, rather than rise into the transcendent, deteriorates into something natural. The individual soul dissolves into the anonymity of the universe, and the personal life into a cosmic life-force. The tone of the individual soul sounds in the rhythm of the universal melody. Much in anthroposophy, in the rhythmic culture, and in other currents of thought take this path. The first way of thinking tears unity asunder, the second negates essential distinctions. In the former, the basic hostile conviction against the body eliminates the possibility of reciprocal impact. In the latter, the life-giving tension between the two is sublated by turning them into the same thing. The former eliminates the understanding that the soul is the *forma* of body; the latter eliminates her as an independent spiritual substance.

In truth, the soul is a spiritual substance. In her being, she transcends matter: in her actions above the chain of natural causes, and free in herself. Between her and the matter of the body, there is an essential difference, which cannot be negated or denied. She is above nature, in her essence independent from the world and therefore capable of ruling over things. She is personal, sprung forth from God's specific creative act. Therefore, she is above the bonds of race and tribe, of community and history. She is God-immediate: an *I* rooted in herself as called upon by God, and ultimately answerable only to him.

The same soul is contemporaneously the essential form of the body. She is the force that forms the matter of the living structure and the integrated causal unity which is the body. Her being and potentialities make up the immaterial essence-image of the body. The soul reveals herself in every line, in every movement, in every measure, in every sense. The soul is the living *entelecheia*[10] of the body.

Therefore, the *formation* of the body is not just a thing of nature comparable to the formation of plants. It has something natural about it, but it is at the same time a personal and ethical thing. It embraces the laws of nature and personal governance, two in one. It unifies the immediate embodiment of the forming principle in the formed matter, although the soul remains independently transcendent. Soul and body form a living unity, the soul internal yet different in nature, struggling by its unique potentialities to overcome and surpass the limitations of the flesh, although sometimes overcome itself.

---

10. MGV note: By *entelechy* Aristotle and the newer philosophies understand the organic view of essence that works in the living and gives special shape to its construction and its particular way of behavior, e.g., the essence of the birch tree or the falcon. See Hans Driesch, *Philosophie des Organischen* [The Philosophy of Organic] (Leipzig: Quelle & Meyer,1930), 391ff.; also Hans André, *The Church as the Nucleus of the Divinization of the World* (Munich, 1921). More recently, see Hedwig Conrad-Martius, *The Self-Construction of Nature: Entelechies and Energies* (1944).

Therefore, the formation of the body becomes the task of the soul. The development of plants and animals is natural, following an inner necessity. Struggle here can only mean the overcoming of external limits of growth. The formation of the body by the soul, rather, embraces a natural event, insofar as it deals with organic growth and an instinctive movement to life, while at the same time, the soul also forms consciously.

As man acts ethically, as he develops habits, as he lives, behaves, and clothes himself, all of these things have a deep impact on his formation. Already at this level, "formation" is not just a necessary event, but even a *task*. The *formatio corporis*, the formation of the body, is something that exceeds mere organic growth: it means the essential ensoulment of the body. This formation does not just have to happen; it has to happen in the right way. The rightly oriented soul must plainly and truly form the body. She herself must be pure, strong, and tender and must make the body into a living expression of such a being. Think of all that the words *posture, self-control, purity, honesty, consideration,* and *sincerity* delineate; we immediately realize that they transcend mere growth, and they stem from a constant intensive effort. Their development passes through the natural, self-possessed uninhibitedness of the child and the tremors of the maturing adolescent to an always more profound understanding and permeation of all bodily being. We venerate the highest achievement of formation in those men who proceed further and arrive at the point of *spiritualization* whereby their bodiliness is governed by soul and spirit to the fullest degree. Only in the *transfiguration* of the resurrected body, which has become fully *spiritual*, a full expression and sense of the soul, fully *light*, as an old parable says, will the soul find fulfillment. This is all to say that the soul, in an always-growing measure of being, will become ever deeper and grow more profound as the *forma corporis*. There is an ever-intensifying spiritual life of the soul entered into a formal relation with the body; the soul will permeate ever-deeper layers of the body in order that she may always shine *brighter* out of the body.

The Christian desires more than mere corporality. He wants to overcome the mighty power of the body by use of his essential freedom, his transcendence over the world, and the omnipresence of God in order to become a real citizen of the spiritual world. This does not mean that he wants to suppress the body or to free himself from it; rather that he wants to make it submissive to the soul and release the soul from the body's governance. He knows the burden of being locked up in the sinful body (Rom 6:6), and is homesick for the wide and pure world of the spirit. However, his last end is not properly a bodiless state as a *purely* spiritual being, but is intended for a spiritualized bodiliness, the assumption of the *spiritual*, the true *spiritual body* that the apostle St. Paul speaks about.[11] The Christian knows about the unity of both. A Christian is not only accused of being an enemy of the body since he is aware of the deep tension between the soul and body in man; but his enemies also accuse him of materializing and reifying spiritual things—a witness to the fact that he has true living freedom. The true Christian attitude is not just the fruit of theoretical speculation; it is, rather, realized through the life of the Christian who can recognize it in whole even through the distractions of quotidian life. Every Christian knows that the soul is the life of the body, its *form*, the grounding for its action and for its unfolding. He sees the body as permeated by the soul in all of its fibers, and he knows that it is the soul's beauty that unfolds in full measure in every line and gesture of the body. He also knows that the soul will immediately lose her nobility if she is reduced to being the mere inner side and rhythm of the body since this tears the God-immediateness and substantial spiritual being away from her, resulting in the loss of the ultimate wholeness and beauty of the body itself.

None of this exhausts the ways in which soul and body relate to one another. Between them is more than a mere life-generating tension. Sin has distraught their relationship. That was the terror of original sin: that it tore a chasm where it was unbearable, in the inner essential relationship between soul and body. We should actually say: between soul and matter, body, since *body* [Leib] already implies spiritual in a certain way.[12] The human body is generated when the soul grasps and forms matter. Now the "flesh has desires against the Spirit" (Gal 5:17) and seeks to overpower it.

---

11. See 1 Cor 15:44. St. Paul contrasts the flesh with the spirit and makes the demand that one overcome the former to reach the latter. Spiritual is not a metaphysical-psychological, but a religious concept. He does not mean a substance, but a state, not the spirit in contrast to the body, but a novel elevation through grace by Christian renewal, a super-formation of the whole, a spiritual-embodied Being in Christ which stands in contrast to the unredeemed state. [MGV note: See Guardini, *The Last Things*, therein especially "The Significance of the Christian Teaching of the Body" (Providence, RI: Cluny Media, 2019), 61ff.]

12. Translator's note: German distinguishes between *body (Körper)* for a merely material being and *body (Leib)* for the body of man, which has a soul.

The *spirit* must fight and defeat the *flesh*, always with the danger that she could destroy it and, therefore, destroy the very foundation of her own action. Yes, the body stands against itself. We experience how urge stands against urge, passion against reason, one creativity against another creativity; but in every desire, there the power of the soul is also, in her plentiful relation to the whole. Distinct areas of life within the whole human experience are posed against each other; thus the soul is also posed—in a terrible way—against herself. She, who is the core of unity and is supposed to create a unified wholeness of life that is essential in all its fullness, carries, conditioned by sin, the battle into her own life.

Man as a whole bears Christian devotion. It is not a "purely spiritual" devotion—what this could look like we do not know. We are not pure spirits, we were not supposed to be, and not even the battle against the body, which is imbued with a desire for freedom, should fool us into thinking this. That is not what we want. The first moment of honesty consists in the acceptance of one's own essence and reliance on it. Our essence is to be human: embodied spirit, ensouled body. Everything we are is human; all that we do is too. God willed it such. The will to perfection does not mean veering away from his idea of our essence into another. This would be both disobedient and foolish since one can only truly live one's own being. We are perfect when we fulfill our essence by becoming an image of God in the fullest sense. Our goal can only be to be fully human. Only the resurrected Christ can reveal to us what "being human" means. That is, Christ who assumed all suffering in his glory. Our earthly bodily state cannot express the fullness of the spiritual life. We know also how deep the disruption of original sin is seated within us, and that is why we reject any superficial belief in progress, which promises that by educational work or social reorganization, the perfect state of life may come to be on earth. Nonetheless, we are faced with the inexhaustible potential of education for the individual within society, society as a whole, and the individual person in his uniqueness, as well as for all types of expressive and "factive" life; we think that God gives us this task. Further, we hope for eternity. That our body may *rise from the dead* is very dear to us and is an almost natural truth. Only in *eternal life* will we be fully human. Now, "what we shall be has not yet been revealed" (1 Jn 3:2), but some words of Sacred Scripture bring us to anticipate the integrity of the transfigured "spiritual body" that will unify the soul to God. Eternal life is called a "song," and a song of praise. Thus, we are not living a religion of pure interiority. The silent internal "word" in which the first concept is formed itself points to an embodiment. If it can unfold completely then it will become an external word, gesture, action, bodily being. It is revealed interiority: a depth filled with life, inner silence that has turned outwards.

Now, there are certainly religious attitudes that emphasize the *spiritual* and *interior* dimension, the wordless prayer in which man strives to God in silence, faces him, or just remains open to God in expectation. The liturgy is different: in it, man in his wholeness is in the center with all his actions and attitudes. At the height of his perfection, man is not supposed to lose his body; quite the opposite, he will become—in the truest sense of the word—ever more human. This means that in the liturgical act his bodiliness strives always more toward interiority and spirituality, while his soul becomes continually more expressed in his body, becoming bodily in a certain sense.

This process has two layers of meaning: from the inside to the outside and from the outside to the inside. It signifies the internal in the external and allows the internal to be read externally. This means that the internal is given by the external and the alien internal is received by the external. It is a symbolic relation in a twofold direction: revealing and recognizing, giving and receiving.

Symbol is not allegory. Allegory connects any kind of meaning to an external common sign, such as justice represented as a woman with blindfolded eyes holding a scale. Such a connection is arbitrary; the whole would retain its sense if the eyes of the person holding the scale were wide open. Symbol on the other hand is linked to the external in such a way that it could not be different.[13] The one belongs to the other by some kind of essential and necessary link.

The apex of the meaning of a symbol is the relation of body and soul. The human body is the analogy[14] of the soul in the sensible-bodily order.

---

13. Of course, one cannot draw a clear line here. Whether one wants to count the handing over of the city keys to the enemy in the first or second group depends upon the feeling of the individual.

14. I use the word *analogy* in the old, precise sense. Accordingly, meaning that the orders of being—i.e., dead, organic, and spiritual being—are in an analogical relation to another. One is related to the other in an ordered fashion despite essential differences between them. The positive content of the superseding level is mirrored by the lower one; the content of the latter is, in turn, received by the higher one.

If one were to express the soul, which is spiritual, in a bodily fashion, then the result would be the human body.[15] This is, in the strictest sense, the meaning of the formula, *anima forma corporis*. The embodied soul, being a living symbol, is itself translated into something bodily. An attentive glance will recognize the soul of the other in his body. It is not his physical actions and self-expression which are responsible for indicating the movement of his soul within; more immediately it may be recognized that the soul realizes itself through the flesh as its symbol: through its very lines, movements, and behaviors.[16] Human attitude is therefore capable of symbol. From the bearer's perspective it is active-symbolic, revealing, and communicative. From the receiver's, it is receptive-symbolic, understanding, and conceiving.

Man is the center of the liturgy as symbol-creator and symbol-receiver. He prays through the unity of body and soul. The movement of his prayer manifests through his ensouled body, and the body expresses the soul. Even the word itself contains this. With the word, there is an embodiment of interiority: man speaks and listens. This is present in every gesture and action: action is the developed embodiment of interiority; man expresses and understands.

Therefore, we are faced with the first task of education in the liturgy: man must become capable of symbol. The essential link between body and soul has been loosened progressively since the Middle Ages. This loosening did not grow out of some kind of asceticism. Genuine asceticism does not want to destroy the body or estrange the soul from it, but wants to bring the body always more under the formative power of the soul. In asceticism, the true relation within man is reestablished, and thus the body is continually more spiritualized. What began in modernity is something completely different. Modernity strives for a *pure* spiritual being, affecting one of the most terrible confusions that has ever plagued the dissent from an integral understanding of man: the *purely spiritual* was sought, and it resulted in something abstract. Embodiment, and therefore symbol, too, were discarded. Almost imperceptibly, the abstract took the place of the

---

15. In the measure in which this can happen, since the higher never fully dissolves into the lower. The whole soul—if I may call it thusly—does not enter the *formatio*. How the transcendence of the soul, its unspoken and hidden part, becomes efficacious cannot be expounded upon here.

16. A symbol with a special character for forming culture appears as soon as an embodiment of this sort becomes pure and necessary through an inner gesture or thing, and must be understood by a people or all of humanity as something definite.

spiritual, the pure concept. The only life-giving force of unity between body and soul was dissolved. The world in which the spiritual was immediately expressed by image, gesture, and construction in the body through actions filled with meaning, customs, and a thousand-fold forms of expression of the spirit revealing itself in interiority filled with meaning, was replaced by a supposedly "spiritual" world. Today we see how "un-spiritual" it was[17]: it was a world of concepts, formulas, apparatuses, mechanisms, and organizations. The target *spirit* disappeared, suffocated by mechanism and the body, and, abandoned by its *forma* ["form," Aristotelian principle], was understood as a merely biological entity.

How poor the culture of modernity is when measured by the yardstick of the true spirit. It is something we can recognize when we compare an old city with its architecture, customs, and order to a modern city.[18] Here the truly *human* action, the symbol, does not find room. We can observe that a thought and a will that raise the claim to be spiritual are merely abstract—that is, as un-spiritual as possible—and will affect as their opposite only a material bodiliness that is no longer human since it is soulless, and therefore inhuman.

The mysterious faculties by which the spiritual is translated into the body and by which every form and gesture become an expression of the spirit, enriching the spirit, instead of manifesting through the ensoulment of the body, waste away. The capacity to make visible and to see, to express, and to understand that which is expressed wanes away. One denies formation. One only understands how to *learn* and to *apply* what has already

---

17. MVG Note: This characterization, "un-spiritual" as used by RG, could be misunderstood. It must be understood in the context of the youth movement against the Rationalism, Technicism, and Progressive Optimism of the end of the nineteenth and beginning of the twentieth century. RG gave this expression of cultural critique in his "Letter from Italy" (published first in *Schildgenossen* in the years 1923–1925 and then with the title *Letters from Lake Como* [Grand Rapids, MI: Eerdmans, 1994], first published in Germany in 1926) an almost classic significance. Even in those texts it is clear that he is not dealing with pessimistic resignation or even romantic backwardness toward an idealized past, but with a forward view in full consciousness of the disappearance of treasured possessions of culture in the formation of the future. The writer does not go against the ratio of—not unbeknownst to the youth movement—irrationalism or *idealism*, or against technology and the machine, in favor of a romantic return to craftsmanship and peasantry. This is evident especially in his later words *The End of the Modern World* (Wilmington, DE: Intercollegiate Studies Institute, 2001;Würzburg, 1964) and *Culture as Work and Threat* (Heidelberg, 1949).

18. MGV note: To illustrate what he means here, we point to the essay of Rudolf Schwarz from around the same time, titled: "Construction Site Germany" in, *Die Schildgenossen*, 12th year, vol. 1, p. 1ff.; and most of all the substantial, but fully forgotten, book by the same author *On the Cultivation of the Earth* (Heidelberg, 1949).

been learned. What rests on musing capability disappears: the imagery of language, the expressive posture of the body, formal dress and living space, a formed way of dealing with one another, game, and dance. Art as an interpretation of being and an elevation of life, as a school of vision and wisdom, disappears. What gets lost, in a word, is living *formation*: the being formed in bodiliness through the spirit and the revelation of the spirit in the body;[19] a *formed* humanity, human culture. Yes, culture, as we have always understood it, disappears.

A natural correlative is the disappearance of the capacity for liturgical action. Here lies the deeply rooted connection: in the measure in which the old attitude is replaced with a new one, living liturgy disappears. Its place is taken by an alleged *internal* and *spiritual* devotion, one that is reduced more and more to the work of a *holiday* and a liturgy that is felt to be merely a *ceremony*. Religious life retreats into the purportedly purely spiritual, but in truth becomes abstract, full of formulas and schemata, and is purely *ritual*. It loses its relation to the inner structure of life. *Formation*

---

19. What do we mean by education today? To us, an educated person is [one] who looks beyond specialist knowledge; [one] in whom knowledge has permeated his or her looking, feeling, judging. An attitude and a possession that are ultimately rooted in knowledge; Rationalism, the legacy of the Enlightenment. Substantial education means more. In a tree of free and strong standing, its being clearly emerges; a buzzard—see him fly, feel the visual power of his circles—can act as a parable for what we mean here. We know that men are not on the same level as trees and birds. Man is free. It is up to him whether he realizes his nature. With part of his being he is beyond the world, he should shape this world from there. He fights, he searches, and carries all the conflict, all the struggles and failures of fighting and searching. All of this is true. Still, for him, too, education is deeply a matter of being alive, not at all of knowledge or performance.

An educated person, in the true sense of the word, is one who is formed out of an inner being, in being, thinking, and doing; he who lives in a community, in a work environment in which this image is revealed—because no one can be educated for himself; but only in community if the atmosphere and building and way of life and people around him are similar. There is no more unpleasant lack of education than the "educated" of our days: educated by the grace of the Enlightenment. The Middle Ages was the last occidental epoch that had a deep, rich, and clear *image*. Already by the Renaissance, image and education in a comprehensive, holistic sense had disappeared. [MGV note: see. Guardini, *The End of Modern World* (New York: Sheed and Ward, 1956)]. Certainly, this destruction also has meaning. It came at the cost of much that is important and precious to us, especially a sense for the dignity and responsibility of the person. Education is also not an ultimate value: duty, honor, love, and every instruction of conscience are above her. We must not become beautiful spirits and connoisseurs, but must endure where we are. All of this is true. But the destruction of education has eaten so deeply into all of this that it threatens our spiritual life. It is no longer a matter of taste, but of existence; and our hope is that a new image is emerging. We see a promising new beginning in the youth movement. We cannot prematurely name and specify what is up and coming out of it and what should remain from it in the coming time. We have to try to stay open-minded and not come to preconceived conclusions about what will pave the way without seeing a fulfillment in a convincing dimension.

is completely absent.[20] Furthermore, everything bodily in religion, culture, rite, and symbol is misunderstood even more; it is not lived in an immediate fashion and not even seen anymore. It becomes something to be done, and it is reduced to an external form that needs to be *absolved*. Although the symbols survive, they lay dusty and soullessly cold. He who would seek to imbue them anew with their due soul would face an arduous task, and should he explain his labors to another, the listener would shudder with the feeling that it would be easier simply to do away with it all.

Here a deep transformation announces itself. *Modernity* has come to an end. The will appears to stand in opposition to the inner orientation of the last century: in the movements for renewal, in the questions of education in the arts and women's education, and in the pedagogical and youth movements, the will to preserve the integrity of the concrete human being starts to appear. A rejection of the untrue, indeed, far-from-reality *spirituality* of the nineteenth century demonstrates! We are embodied spirits, concrete human beings. Yet we observe the rejection of naturalistic materiality and the materialism of the same century in which men so revoltingly boasted of evolving from an animal!

In each of our bodies a spiritual, God-immediate soul lives. A new attitude is starting to ripen in which a new culture will be born—but it only will when it has found God and held him fast. The Body Culture and Dalcroze Eurhythmics[21] movements want the same thing. As strange as it may seem and as disoriented as it may be, therein lies a desire for a truly ensouled body, an image and expression of the spirit, the longing for a fully human being and life. In addition, as long as this movement is not led astray by the winds and fancies of some contemporary fashion, then it will

---

20. To say it again, this should not misjudge what it contained in value, since every era has its meaning and mission before God. The modern sharpening of the person-consciousness, the refined feeling for the concrete and historical-special, the strength of development of the responsibility have brought meaningful values to the Christian religion, as well as to the modern sense for mathematical accuracy and technical fidelity. But the effect of special forces and attitudes is always bought with the stunting of others; in this case, the ones we have been talking about here. Our considerations have nothing to do with the question as to what people of that time count morally and religiously before God.

21. Translator's note: Dalcroze eurhythmics is a developmental approach used to teach music to students. It was developed in the early twentieth century by Swiss musician and educator Émile Jaques-Dalcroze. Dalcroze eurhythmics teaches concepts of rhythm, structure, and musical expression using movement, and is the concept for which Dalcroze is best known.

Body Culture or Körperkultur is an umbrella term for an early twentieth century societal reform movement in Germany that focused on reviving the body by healthy activity in nature. The movement was critical of industrialization, materialism, and urbanization of human life.

reawaken the faculties, which reveal the spirit in the body and are able to read and express the bodily aspect of the spiritual core.

In the measure in which this new attitude is formed, the understanding of the Christian-Catholic essence is also born anew. When dealing with man, Christian teaching regains actuality. Only now can Nietzsche and his struggle against everything pertaining to Christianity be fully understood because only now do some human persons, and quite a few of them, resonate his thoughts. Often the Catholic is understood as the *pagan*, even though the ideas, which feed accusations of paganism, are in fact so deeply "human." What is at stake is the critical choice between the person being elevated through grace in Christ or striving independently to become *super-human* and *divine*; between being reborn in the *new man* by losing oneself in God or wanting to be autonomous, standing for oneself and wanting to be *like God* by one's own capacity. *Paganism* and Catholic Christianity are profoundly related to one another. The former is all natural in an open state of nature, taking nature as the standard, ignorant of a super-worldly and personal God; the latter is the fulfilled Christianity, which assumes everything natural into the supernatural and reveals itself as open to all being. Their attitudes are related: they are both open to all that is real and void of subjectivism; they are lacking the willful selection of some parts of the whole of reality. Both also see that man is in the center and want to address the questions he raises.[22]

Herein lies the tragedy of every paganism: It cannot do justice to nature as mere nature. Only when that which is transcendent over nature gains a foothold—culminating with Christ—can nature be fully assumed and unfolded. *Nature* in itself is something questionable. It demands essential perfection out of itself, but can only reach it when rooted in *grace*. Only in the transcendent super-natural can nature unfold its own potential. If it closes itself into itself, then it sinks down into the sub-natural. Nature has the choice only between being super-natural or sub-natural. That is the antinomy of the natural, which at its core must be in the center of every philosophy of culture, which seeks to be true to reality. We know "that creation itself would be set free from slavery to corruption and share in the glorious freedom of the children of God. We know that all creation is

---

22. We should not forget that false spirituality and exaggerated asceticism, stinginess and closed mindedness, are too often to be found in Christian life; here we are dealing with a fundamental attitude.

groaning in labor pains even until now" (Rom 8:21–22). In the pagan attitude, which stands open to concrete reality, there lies a great temptation to forget that supernaturally borne nature is truly *natural* and that mere nature immediately sinks into the state of sub-nature. Therefore, we must now qualify what we said about humanity in paganism. It only extends to a certain limit since to be human also essentially means being oriented toward God and his sovereign grace.[23] This is indeed *real*; it is above all. An autonomous focus on this-worldliness is against man's essence and therefore non-human. Even if the Christian gives up all of his formation for the sake of Christ, he is still incommensurably more human than the pagan who closes himself up in a this-worldly autonomy and thereby—biblically speaking—loses his soul. What I mean is very clear: what the Christian has in common with the pagan is an open attitude toward all being.

We witness the rise of a new paganism. Christian tradition has lost all of its meaning on a very broad spectrum.[24] It seems that many people have lost their Christian heritage and returned to being essentially pagan—as far as that is even possible after so many centuries of Christian history. This paganism is not simply a decay of, nor apathy or animosity toward, religion as it was in previous centuries. It is embodied by people who have high ideals, who are pure and well intended. It is paganism with open eyes and the will for an oriented soul in an oriented body; it proclaims an integral humanity, which it wants to see lived across the whole world. This paganism carries a soul schooled, deepened, and refined by two millennia of Christian education. A great decision rises before us, and Goethe and Nietzsche have prepared it: We need to choose between *Rome and Athens* or the *Cross*, which is "a stumbling block to Jews and foolishness to Gentiles" (1 Cor 1:23).

The enemy of Christian Catholicism is paganism. Both want—with the delineation just made—integrity. They both embrace the entire breadth of natural being. Through Christ, the Catholic Christian is able to overcome the world and reform it. The world is the fullness of things, while the fullness of man is his foundation to establish the kingdom of God after all is redeemed through the Cross. For the *pagan* the world itself becomes

---

23. MGV note: See Romano Guardini, *Man Can Only Be Discovered by the One Who Believes in God* (Würzburg, 1965).

24. MGV note: See Romano Guardini, *Faith in Our Time* (Würzburg, 1962).

divine in a certain way. The pagan does not know, in fact he denies, the personal God and Creator, and he denies the fact of the *Cross*.

The decision to follow either Christianity or paganism will be acted out in the special realm with which we are dealing here. All those movements of which we have spoken affect a new humanization of man; they wake the faculties and powers that have withered hitherto. The question remains: Does this happen in order to accord them to God that we may regain a truly Christian way of life and a truly Christian culture? In order that in the deepest sense a liturgical formation may seize our whole life and transform it?[25] On the other hand, are they movements by which the merely human arises, where man becomes the *super-human* and a *kind of god?* In being one with nature and the cosmos, should man become a *devoted pagan?* One must choose between Catholic liturgy or pagan nature and world religion.

For us the answer to this question is clear: here all forces and faculties that have withered since the origin of modernity arise. Here a truly liturgical attitude is possible once again.

This gives us our first practical task: carried by the inner transformation of our time, we must relearn how to stand in a religious relationship as full human beings. We must learn, too, to pray with the body. The posture of the body, our gestures, and our actions must become directly religious once more. We must learn to express interiority in our outward appearance and to read the internal by the external. In other words, once more must we become capable of symbol. If the young person grows in the right way and in the right environment with nature, and if he forms his body in hiking, games, and exercise; if he works with his mind as well as with crafts; then his honesty will teach him to accept with seriousness the weight of the word [symbol]. He will feel what it means to deal with others according to custom and form. He will learn to dress and to form instruments of work and form his environment in general. He will become lord over his body, as is the sense of holistic formation. He will see the growing correlations between soul and body, forms and movements (the measure of his being); then he will develop the right natural predispositions for the correct liturgical attitude. Once one generation has established balance in

---

25. MGV note: Here *liturgical* is understood in a broader sense, which can be seen more clearly from what follows. A sacralization of that which we understand as the profane is not meant here.

all things, overcoming the obstacles posed against them; when this exercise begins in early adolescence, thus seizing the person's being in its first stages of growth; and once this formation occurs repeatedly through multiple generations, then one's being and instinct will form a serious and steadfast legacy.[26] Particularly because of our Christian sense, we will not discard these new currents. We will prudently deal with them, and we will measure them with our spirits and the principles of faith and tradition. At the same time, we will recognize what in them is similar to Christianity, try to foster it, and implement it in our liturgical culture. To this general musing on formation has to be now added the particular: unmediated education to foster the right body-soul attitude toward the symbol. This must begin with the child. The child must learn—and how easily this is done!—to join all powers of seeing and crafting in his religious life. His educator must introduce liturgical actions and attitudes to him attentively so that the child understands the natural sense of movement and action in each given moment and embraces the proper sense of the action and its link to the religious content in its full potential and essence. The child should experience how it is translated into a living external form.[27]

We can speak for example of elemental liturgical gestures, the simple movements and actions that are—and I will not be able to address this issue in a more profound way—partly of human nature, but find their essential fulfillment in the liturgy.

This sort of introduction must happen in a moment of receptivity, when the soul is awake and the body is sensitive and attentive to imagery. When a mother is truly a mother to her child and a teacher is truly a teacher, then they will recognize the dawn of this perfect moment.

Most of this will happen by the living example of the family and community. By this the child will grow into the sense and order of liturgical events and action as if it were the most natural thing in the world.

---

26. MGV note: Here we can see how musical education should be dear to the Church and her educators. It remains true: *gratia supponit naturam*—without such education that begins in childhood, growing to have a liturgical approach as spoken of by the author is scarcely possible.

27. MVG note: In this context, we should point to the attempts of religious-cultic education which Maria Montessori had set out to realize in her Roman orphanages.

I have given practical indications for this and the subsequent chapter in the booklet *Sacred Signs* (St. Louis: Pio Decimo Press, 1956).[28] What is written here are some snippets whose fragmentary nature I am well aware of. It will all most likely have to come together afterwards in the developed whole. At least it may inspire improvement. We tell the children, "God is so great, and we humans are so small and so poor when facing him. When we face him in all readiness, then it is like saying to him: 'I am something good; just as much as you!' You have to be humble, you have to make yourself small—see, like this!" Then you let the child kneel down. When the hour is right and the teacher is authentic, the child will never forget it. God's magnitude, one's own smallness, the sense of humility, and the act of kneeling mold together into a whole and single unity. You can explain it similarly by comparing the greetings of your own culture and the act of kneeling in front of God in church.

Or you say, "When a man speaks, then his hands speak as well. Look how naturally they move as he speaks. The hands say so much! Similarly, when you speak with the good God, then your hands must speak as well . . . Like this . . . !" And you fold them. They can speak with "tenseness and an expression of interiority, do you feel it?" And you weave the fingers together. *Or very seriously* you press the hands flat against each other. "Is that not beautiful?" Then you show him hands folded sloppily and folded with care. You ask, "Do you realize how uneducated these hands are? How lazy and ungodly?" This, in short, is a primal phenomenon in the relation between body and soul: Whatever is *more* or *less* valuable in the spiritual realm corresponds to the bodily *higher* and *lower*. Similarly the image of the most perfectly whole—that which is closer to God—is expressed in the higher. When a mother takes her child into the church at the right hour, walks slowly up the stairs into the church and says, "Now we climb up . . . up into the church . . . to God," then the child will correlate the bodily climbing with the spiritual ascension to God.

The sign of the cross can likewise become a deep experience. A mother speaks of Jesus, the Savior, to the child. She tells him what he suffered on the Cross because he loved us: "In the sign of the Cross, the Lord is present. In it, he inclines himself down to you, and he takes you up into

---

28. MVG note: In the mentioned *Sacred Signs*, RG has given an elementary cultic education, which may need some updating, but is overall not obsolete.

his arms because he loves you so much. Do it now . . . very slowly . . . very wide . . . from the forehead to the chest, from one shoulder to another . . . the Lord blesses you, he blesses all of you: your head, and your heart, your limbs, your body, and your soul. He makes it so that you fully are his; he wants to make all of you holy."

Many things can become a liturgical experience. For example, the way one walks in church as an expression of solemn movement in the face of God; standing in church as a sign of readiness; the way the sinner strikes his breast, taking position against himself in the face of God and punishes himself because he has failed in the love of God; and much more.

The simple act of climbing up can become a more intricate movement. For example, the procession as the act of the greatest, most solemn joy, as a confession to the world, or as an accompaniment of the Lord through his own kingdom; the gestures made while receiving the most holy nourishment; one's attitude toward confession, toward the Eucharist, and so forth.

It always comes back to the central issue: to emphasize the content of the given, holy action in its most essential characteristic offered to the receptive child in the proper and appropriate form is what counts. Furthermore, it is necessary to bring to one's own mind the given gesture, posture, or action, in its specific bodily dimension and quality, to act it out beautifully and fully and then merge both into one. One has to be attentive that the individual action be performed slowly, authentically, and with full consciousness. It should not be performed too often, otherwise it will become careless. The action should not be done in the wrong moment, otherwise its internal content and essence will not fit the environment or occasion. The observing child would then either feel confused and reluctant, or will act it out, but then the external form will be ill-fitting to the internal content. In this case something would be destroyed that was central—that is, the essential expression. This expression is not dependent, at least not solely, on the educator, but relies on formation by the divine worship of the community. Here lie urgent tasks, which require keen attention.

Man and Thingness[29]

The fullness of the spiritual cannot be sufficiently conveyed by consideration of the body's expression by faculties, movements, limbs, and contours. The human being expands by taking on the things of his environment, extending his bodily dimension by the incorporation of exterior things. In the first place, these expressive possibilities of form, of its measure, proportions, and movements, will be enriched by clothing.

Further, the lines and movements of the limbs extend through tools. In this way, the form and movement of a given limb is enriched. The performing hand's expression is expanded when it holds a bowl; the power of a punch is strengthened when a hammer is held. Moreover, from the beautiful contrast between utensils in their stiff forms and living bodies with limbs come new possibilities of expression.

The figure is framed by a certain environment that is conscientiously formed with chairs, tools, and ornaments. Expressive actions are ordered according to their natural beginning, end, and duration. Something meaningful manifests through a double ordering: the objective world with its immeasurable space, continuously flowing time, and unexpected fullness of beings forms for man an impenetrable width, an all-encompassing current, and a perplexing whole of figures and events that is insurmountable by the soul. In his nature, man's powers fall short of the task of ensouling and forming this world. He loses himself in it. Living in him is the audacity to venture into the endlessness with its insurmountable fullness. But in order to embark on his journey, he needs a home base—a place at which to start and to end. He wants a point of reference by which he can join the newly discovered and that which he has overcome. He wants a livable *human world* within the alien and strange cosmos. Thus he makes his horizon denser and reduces larger confusion into a limited concept that he can govern. At first this is a closed systematically formed space. In it, the measure of things and their service to life reigns: things to use, places to be,

---

29. Translator's note: The original is *dinglich*, which is more than physical. RG seems to reference a dense philosophical term *Ding* ("thing") which is more than "physical" ("material"). His use is reminiscent of Kantian and especially Husserlian phenomenology. Therefore, I chose *thingness* to emphasize the essential characteristic of the things, as pertaining to the substance of a work, separate from what is conveyed, since that is what RG focuses on throughout.

ornaments to beautify. And the acts that happen in this space are tied to a very specific, measured time. By man's choice and ordering of parts within the greater whole of the room that he fashions, the space comes to represent in a condensed form the insurmountable fullness of the cosmos. This construct, its form and its space, its useful instruments and its beauty, man can ensoul along with time as its measure and the connection of the comforting cyclical return of its fragmented events. He can imbue it with a spirit and involve the expressive feature of his body. He can also experience the whole along with all of its parts—the edifice with all of its possibilities of expression such as its mass, space, and thing—as the extension of his personal capacities of expression. In the same way, time and its rhythm are only an extended *body* and a means for the soul to express itself.

Yet something else happens: As soon as the environment swells in measure and form, it grows beyond submission to the practical and homely expectations of man. It wins its own subsistence and imposes itself on man with ever greater force. He senses that the object as such stands before him. He does not just feel. This is how I am; but also, there is another around me, opposed to me. He senses the objective breadth of being, the fullness of things, the possibility of the order of events, and himself standing in midst of them. He senses requirements imposed upon him to which he has to submit. Body, clothing, and instruments easily become instruments of the pure self-expression of man. As a whole, the formed space and time gain a consciousness under an objective reality and have such a force that the will of the ego to express itself surrenders under the overpowering weight of their call to service. We will have to say more about this later.

This fullness of space and time cannot be unfolded limitlessly. How much the individual can cope with regard for his capacities for formation and expression becomes a question of personal cultural power and maturity.

Living means not just experiencing the limits and instrumental value of an interior space, but also sensing the inner value of ornaments and useful instruments, and experiencing them in relation to one's feelings. The stronger the cultural force of the individual, the more he possesses this skill-to-inhabit. A house, a room is only "possessed" when the space and the walls, the seats and the ornaments are experienced in a lively way. A house as an organism of rooms, household goods, and furniture only becomes a home when the person connects his sense of being to it, when he carries in himself a sentiment for living being. This is the cultural force, which determines the extent to which an individual or a family can live in a garden with its value of use and beauty, or more in a park or a large estate. Herein lies the organic measure of a living right to possess one's own which obviously no law can prescribe.[30] The situation is similar with the order of houses, streets, and squares, as well as the structural order of public buildings. The proper sense of a "home town" can only emerge in a city, which is integrally and orderly lived-in such that as a whole it becomes an organ of self-expression.[31] The same applies to one's native country when it has grown into the whole reality of life. From this point of view, hiking, for example, gains a new and deeper meaning. One's powers of ensoulment extend over the whole land. When hiking, one's personality grasps forests, moors, mountains, rivers, cities, and towns. One sees their expanse and details, industries and farms, peoples in their individuality and in relation to others, and places them into the field of expression of one's own living being until the point is reached when one can say out of the innermost depth of truth: my home—that is me. I cannot be without it, but it can also not be without me. I only can briefly touch upon the strength with which the city, the land, and the home are present before me and how much they foster the fullness of my self-fulfillment by opening my soul and demanding her truthful service in return. How deep can the love for one's homeland become! How much can we grasp that we must serve the land, which nourishes our soul and gives its words a rich realization; it speaks to us of free and plentiful life!

All of this comes to its own in the religious context. Here we have formed matter, the formalized space of the divine dwelling and all of its liturgical instruments. This space is ordered according to the elements of the cult (narthex, sanctuary, most holy tabernacle, orientation, right and left . . .), as well as due to art. In it, sacred actions are instantiated *according to their time*! It embraces the fullness of its temporal elements with their rhythm according to year, season, month, week, day, and hour. Just as the hour of Mass integrates itself into the week of the year, in the same way

---

30. That everyone should only possess the same amount is evidently false. However, our sense for justice demands that no one person should have all possessions. We feel uneasy when someone possesses more than what he can deal with during his lifetime—save limits that respect for others demands.

31. For example, see the speech of Goethe about Frankfurt, in *Poetry and Truth*.

the space of the divine temple fills a place in the special extension of churches: the parish church is the daughter of the bishop's cathedral, and all churches gather around the original basilica of the Savior in Rome. Further, all sacred spaces depend on the parish church: the cemetery, perhaps additional chapels and shrines. Sacred space also unfolds into the profane by processions, devotional visits, and pilgrimages. In this, the profane space is ordered according to the sacred space. The totality of the fullness of this reified, special, and chronological occasion of expression is involved in the inner soul-body relation of the liturgy. What happens in the soul—rebirth out of God in Christ through the Holy Spirit, the life of the Reborn One through God-given forces—is expressed in the body, through its use and in its way. This opens further possibilities: the soul is prompted to express itself in manifold ways. Often, what needs to be expressed is awakened thusly for the first time. This expression by the person acting is self-revelation, while for the person who witnesses the expression it is a message, which reveals the innermost core of expression to his eyes and ears. This expression—and I pick up on an earlier line of thought—is not just self-revelation, but is service. Because of the severity of divine space and sacred times, man realizes how he is not facing an unformed meaningless chaos, which invites him to give it meaning. He sees himself faced with the *thingness*[32] of spaces, times, and things. Even his own body has an objective lawfulness in itself. What he wants to express is in the deepest sense objective because what he wants to express does not solely rely on his creative arbitrariness. His religious life is formed by thoughts, truths, and realities, which are independent of him in their revelation and given to the Church. Life-events are virtually prescribed for him.

What we have called "expression" transforms into something else: from mere creative spontaneity into something universal. It turns into obedience, action, and *service*. Service to God, toward his revelation, law, and truth. Service to his creation with its objective laws and essences. Finally, service to one's own being, which acts according to its own proper laws which one ought not to abuse.

---

32. Translator's note: As mentioned in note 29, the original is *dinglich*, which is more than physical. RG seems to reference a dense philosophical term *Ding* ("thing") which is more than "*physical*" ("*material*"). His use is reminiscent of Kantian and especially Husserlian phenomenology. Therefore, I chose *thingness* to emphazise the essential characteristic of the things, as pertaining to the substance of a work, separate from what is conveyed, since that is what RG focuses on throughout.

In this way, liturgical expression grows to become a universal behavior that is subjective-individual, creative self-expression, and at the same time objective-universal, disciplined, and directed toward service. Simultaneously, obedience and creativity are fluid and orderly in their conjunction. Uniting ruling and service, creativity and obedience together form a greater unity that St. Benedict calls the *Opus Dei*.[33] In it, man continues creative work; all things become the substance and instrument of a higher order: the divinely reincarnate world of the Christian life. This creation and revelation is at the same time docile service. It does not happen arbitrarily, but in a spirit of obedience—obedience to the objective laws that God himself has given through natural revelation and that speak through us in the essences of things and by supernatural revelation in Christ. In doing this, a rebirth occurs "for which all creation yearns" (Rom 8:22). In it man is, as the apostle Paul says, Lord of all creation, because creation serves him in his expression of the mystery of mysteries: the life of the Christian soul. At the same time, he is the *servant of all creation* because he does not act autocratically, but obediently to the law, which God put in the nature of things and in their end, which is itself ordered toward God.

All of this gives the present day a feeling of alienation. Antiquity stood lively in its relation toward creation, as is evident with the mystery cults.[34] The Middle Ages too were marked by this, as we can still experience in the cathedrals, unsurpassed in preponderance though from a time called *dark* by the pretentious Enlightenment. All of that was a means of expressing the mighty fullness of religious experience; it is a world full of symbol in its highest form with clear unity that must be constructed. Cathedrals, the *Summa theologiae*, legends, lore, and world histories are unities in which the all-embracing self-revelation of the Christian spirit permeates every detail, every thing and event surrounding humanity.[35]

Concomitantly, the whole world was consecrated in the liturgy, in the fullness of liturgical action, as one can still witness in consecrations, concentrated around sacrifice and sacrament, unfolding in the great order

---

33. Divine *work*. This word has two senses: work enacted by God and work done for God.

34. See the work of Odo Casel, "Liturgy as Celebration of the Mystery," *Ecclesia orans* IX (Freiburg, 1922).

35. MGV note: This is not essentially changed even if the dimension of knowledge of this self-revelation has—for the modern person—lost its meaning for the most part, due to historical and natural sciences.

of space and time. And not only was this true of all that was contemporary, but also all that had passed was assumed—after all, what is legend but the inclusion of the personalities and events of history into Christian self-expression? There was deep interiority and a rich fullness of expression. Man was aware of the super-worldly quality of his soul, and man was at the same time a living organ of the world in touch with all creatures. He had a deep understanding of the world; yet he was only able to extend to such a depth by strong asceticism. Wide, delicate bodiliness was ensouled and open to revelation. At the same time, man stood in and experienced with clarity an indubitable order. A great *service* happened, in truth, a *service toward all creatures*. Man had not fallen into the dumb bondage to things, but rather was free and creative in the service of creation, in a state in which all things spoke and announced the supernatural world of grace and love. All began to shine with inner light. Everything began to radiate with inner light, a transfiguration, a striving upward. Enjoying such strength and color in his bodily aspect, man's being was saturated with unchallenged power, and at the same time, all things around him, too, glowed in transfiguration!

Observant and listening, obedient and at the same time very free, the Christian walked through the world, open and full of powerful creative energy. He himself was free, and he freed all things through his humble service, which in turn freed the deep-seated voice of his essence beginning to proclaim itself. How human was life, and how high did it rise into the sacred height of spiritualization! What followed was dissolution. It would take too long to express the whole path of man finally losing the unity and cohesion of all reality. He became the man of the modern city, a man of concepts and formulas. He lost his immediate sense of things, his feel for their fullness, and the deep, intensive reality resting within them. The faculties by which he was connected to reality shriveled; his whole life became "artificial." The order of life was reversed. Natural rhythms of day and night, and the seasons too, were no longer experienced. Space became insurmountable, unable to be penetrated by man's spirit. Man lost the capacity to live with things and to express his own essence in using them. At the same time, man lost himself to things to an extent to which the people of the Middle Ages never did. He could not fill them anymore with his spirit and soul; he took them as mere matter, as objects of property, of making, of researching. In the same measure they gained power over him.

His technical governance of the world became his inner abandonment toward the world.

On the religious plane, this was expressed in the development of the demand for *purely spiritual*, purely interior devotion. The thingly, the image, the concrete appearances of things in the world were removed from the realm of the religious; man became alienated from the image, himself growing emptier, abstract, ever poorer. And sacredness left the outside world. The world became ever more *profane*, always less spiritual and more akin to quotidian life. Through one century after another it was deported to matter, benefit, and will to possession. All those religious powers that can only live in physical expression had to wither. Spiritual life needs the fullness of the thingness in order to unfold. Surely therein lies the danger of externalization, should its content gain too much of an external and thingness character.[36] However, without it religion cannot live long, and every attempt to make it purely *interior* and *spiritual* leads to its withering away even further. The new forms of religious life became ever poorer in image, and forms that were filled with reality, these became ever more conceptual, schematic, and artificial. At the same time, man forgot to master things according to God's calling, and as a consequence, they became overpowering. They could not be mastered ethically, practically, or religiously. And something else waned, too: Man lost the power of pure expression. He lost the power to speak God's revelation in things and to hear his message. He unlearned purposeless service in the truth of God, pure representation and worship, the veneration of God without any objective, reverence which grows out of the free joy of fullness in divine glory; that form of religion in which all motion is saturated by worship, gratitude, and without any purpose save for the "glory of God" (1 Cor 10:31). Man's own aims became overpowering together with their formulas and methods. An ethical-moral character evermore colored religion; it became prompting to right action.

---

36. Translator's note: See my comment in note 29 above. I think what RG tries to say in these sentences is that religious sentiment experienced a development which was calling for something removed from matter (in the Platonic sense, where all matter is evil), that is, it was calling for something purely spiritual. Therefore, all that had to do with matter—the physical, the image, the appearances—(as opposed to the ideas) were abolished to "purify" spirituality, as if human beings could live a spirituality that is totally matter-free, like the angels.

The *Opus Dei* kept losing its meaning for man; it was supplanted by the *opus hominis*. The purposeless ensoulment of all things, their transfiguration by man reborn in God, and the revival of the world into a new, redeemed creation, without any other purpose than that it just *be*—all of that faded into the background to make room for the ethical-practical goals of religious industriousness, discipline, and organization.

Liturgical life grew ever bleaker. More and more it was understood as mere *edification*, mere ornament, often a *superfluous waste of time*, or even as the materialization of religion—or however else an ignorant tongue could describe it.

Yet an opportunity has already announced itself. Something awakens that I have already described elsewhere:[37] the consciousness of the reality of things, seen from the source of their features. Consciousness awakens to see the fullness of things, their all-encompassing and all-permeating order. Once again, man recognizes himself as a *small world* within a *large world*; he stands facing and engaging in the fullness and breadth of the latter. He senses his original human relation to things, the root of any true understanding of what symbol is. To everything, man says: "*That*, I am not. I am *other*, more immediate to God, connected to him and at his service. Nothing can express my soul; in no earthly thing can it be expressed. She is entirely alienated here, only wandering; my home is there above." But at the same time, he feels related to all things because the things also carry in themselves the divine image of the same God, out of which man comes. In God, all things are related, and man is destined to gather all their essences in himself and unify them in a living relationship toward them. "A great thing is the soul," says St. Bonaventure together with the masters of the Middle Ages; "she is destined to be impressed onto the whole world." When man encounters a thing, an ambivalent sensation of alienation as well as a special relation to it arises simultaneously in him. Something connected to the thing calls out to him; he responds and strives to express his own essence in its form. This is how the symbol comes to be. Between man and the thing, that which is similar from the side of man calls the form [Gestalt] of the other toward himself and turns it into the material expression of his interiority, while what is different stands guard

---

37. Romano Guardini, *The Meaning of the Church* (Providence, RI: Cluny Media, 2018), chapter 1.

between them such that man does not fall or find himself absorbed into the thing, maintaining a distance, and thusly power and clarity, toward the form. Otherwise, original solitude would rather turn into melting together with no form coming from it. The other would posit its form into nothingness. Only when both are together can they create meaning, symbol. True symbol means proportionality instead of mistaken identity; it means meaning instead of evanescent nothingness.

In the previous section, "Soul and Body," we said that the deepest meaning to be found in the cultural movement of our day may be that we will be filled anew with humanity and strive for the true expression of human nature. Not toward the spirit and not toward the animal, but toward what we truly are: human beings—soul that forms the body, and body that is permeated by the soul and is expressed in revelation. We ought to become essential. For us, this means to be truly human. Our relations and actions in life, as well as our customs in society, our customs in labor, and our joy itself, must become essentially human. There ought to be an *anima*, which is the *forma corporis*. True spirit and also real body. How adequately the soul forms the body will be the measure of expression and clothing. The same spirit also strives toward the true reality of things. Formulas and concepts—in their rightful sense and validity—have barred our view from reality as a whole. We do not think with lively imaginations, but by signs, and in systems of extracted features signifying things, like pieces of cash, which take on value although they are valueless in themselves. We have not felt the shock of reality with an open heart or felt the uniqueness of things' reality. Now the will arises anew to see things instead of concepts, to think and speak of realities and not mere words. To deal with the whole world in its fullness and force, in all its hardness, and in fruitful confrontation, is given to us as a task once again. Our task is to stand in awe before the intrinsic sense of things; to call them by name, as they are; to hear their expression, and at the same time to target them with the will of formation. Man's approach to things has to be with observing eyes and listening ears. He should not do violence to things, but he should completely involve them in his way of expressing the soul in the body.[38] In a very deep sense, the soul is called to be the *forma* of the world outside.

---

38. MGV note: In this context, we can also see the pedagogical intention of Maria Montessori; and F. J. J. Buytendijk's beautiful book *Education to Humility* (Leipzig, 1928).

This does not mean a pantheistic dissolution of one into the other; rather that while man is alien to things, he is also mysteriously so close that he may use them for his expression.

This is just as much the task of the creative formation of symbols: man should not do violence to things, but unlock their deepest essence by revealing himself in them. As it is the essence of art to reveal man's inner essence and express it, through art's purposelessness and purity of form, precisely in the revelation of what the thing represented is, so the essence of the true symbol is the mutual essence-image of the expressing human being and the essence of the thing that is expressed.

Here lies the point of departure for the renewal of liturgical formation. We have already seen how the liturgy fulfills the work of formation. Man expresses himself through things. The *anima* becomes the form of the thing, grasps it, and draws it into a relation of expression with the body through clothes, instruments, space, and time as well as by the action that happens with it. Our acts sprout out of awe and are pruned by obedience to the demands of the essence of the thing; it will not be abused but is transfigured by affirmation of its essential core. It is a truly unique action: the soul frees the essence of the thing and uses it for a higher purpose of imagination; it becomes freer to unfold itself precisely because it becomes a means to express the life of grace of the Christian soul. Think of the sacraments. Let us deepen the richness in meaning that water has in the liturgy. In the prayers of its blessing, its demonic duplicity is revealed; we can sense it in restless currents, in its swirling and rushing: refreshing but menacing, mild yet dreadful, clear and mysterious in one. There is something magical, alluring, even evil in it. Whosoever does not sense this does not understand what nature is. The liturgy knows this and knows that the same powers reside in the soul itself. That which is ungodly lives and works in all of nature. For something to be suitable for God, it must undergo deep cleansing. In the liturgy, we experience the deep duplicitousness of nature, the might of the elemental powers, and we ask ourselves where its dubious origin lies. We sense how little we actually are self-aggrandizing, since we realize that it is the deepest part of the essence of creation to *belong* to *someone*. We never belong to ourselves. If we do not abandon ourselves to God, then we will necessarily descend into the ungodly. In consideration of things, the liturgy has the sense of taking them from the earthly hand to bring them to the rightful hand, to take them out of the hand of the "Lord of the world" (Jn 12:31) and to bring them into the Father's. Thus, water can become something pure, become "useful, humble, precious, and pure" (Liturgy of the Easter Vigil). It purifies and is fruitful; it becomes a living symbol of supernatural life. We invite you to read the wonderful words of the blessing of holy water, and how the holy water font becomes a "cradle of heavenly fruitfulness."

The same is true for all other materials: fire, oil, salt, ash, wax—they are presented to us so that we may come to sense their essential fullness, especially in the moment when they become signs of the supernatural abundance of the Spirit. Liturgical formation must begin here. What is the aim of this new formation? To guide the children away from the mere use of concepts into a living exchange with things; a life within reality. Mountain hiking is of such a nature. We must create a new awakened feeling for material authenticity, for an essential formation, crafting and high-quality work, for a personal creation of artistic work in cloth, instrument, and living space. Formation aims for the turning toward the concrete as in philosophy and pedagogy—everything is prepared in view of this. Here is championed the basic foundation for the renewal of the authentic liturgical expression of the thing.

Then a total formation will not be a challenge.[39]

A teacher could explain the nature of water to the child accordingly: First, he says that water is both essential for life and treacherous, even dangerous as a mere element; it has an ungodly, alluring sense of magic (i.e., in the solitude of a lone lake or the swirling of a river). Second, the teacher can unlock what *consecrating* the water means; explain the intention that it become *holy*. He can explain the life-giving nature of water by taking a fresh drink on a hot hiking day, or describe how when—after a time of drought—the rain returns and invigorating scents fill the air and rejuvenate all. The child's understanding will follow: how water, as an expression of the current fullness of supernatural life, becomes grace. The use of water makes sense when consecrated, since the mere-natural was made fit for God's kingdom. In baptism, this secret fruitfulness is revealed. From there the instruction leads—always mindful of the simple comprehension of a

---

39. Translator's note: see Guardini, *Sacred Signs*.

child—to the silent mystery of the motherly womb, which gives natural life, and finally to the final mystery of the divine womb, in which rebirth to new life begins "out of water and spirit" (Jn 3:5). Now even the daily use of holy water when crossing oneself will gain new meaning: purification and rejuvenation.

Plentiful is the symbolism of fire and light. Once again, discovery begins with the natural element. Brought from a rock during the Easter Vigil, fire has an evil, destructive, and elementally fierce aspect, which can only be half contained by man. Then, once consecrated, it is transformed into an analogy of heavenly heat and divine glow, which becomes love and truth: *Lumen Christi*. From there follows the rich symbolism of light, such as fire burning before the altar.

The candle, symbol of the free, subconscious personality of man, is held by the hand, given and offered as a component of actions of personal sacrifice (vows of baptism, first Communion at the Table of the Lord, the consecration of a virgin) since it represents the agent making the sacrifice (as in last rites, the viaticum). The burning candle becomes an expression of one's willingness for self-sacrifice, and stands evident before God to be consumed at his will. A radiant example of this is the Easter candle, a symbol of Christ, who is both Person and Sacrifice in the fullest sense.

Then there is incense as a symbol of ascending prayer, linen on the altar as a symbol of purity, and various vestments and instruments. The sanctuary too can be explained in this way: first the step, which leads "up" to God's dwelling place, followed by the gate [in the communion rail], which both separates the holy place from the "market" and marks the boundary of the inner space. The same is true of the interior space in which the awareness of one's body swells to fill the space while, at the same time, the feeling of the whole world enters the body. There is the experience of silence and keeping quiet, then the sounds of the organ and the bell. The sound of the bell leads one back out into the world that is, in turn, sanctified by the holy house of God. The space within the church stands in relation to the field of God outside, with the cathedral in the city of the bishop, and chapel and pilgrimage sites out in the country. This all is connected with the mother of all churches, the original Basilica of the Most Holy Redeemer in Rome. Procession and devotional visits consecrate the land proceeding from the church.

It remains invariably central that one maintain a view of the natural essence of the thing present, and speak of it through a sensitive approach, and experience it in itself. Next ranks how it relates to the expression of the soul in the body, and finally how it becomes the carrier of the supernatural fullness of meaning. One cannot force this formation; we have to wait for the hour of receptivity to arrive. One cannot just explain that this element means this or that; it is also unwise to link artificial concepts with similarities in meaning though they do not actually belong to one another. One has to listen to the essence and show how something interior becomes *body*, how form reveals that which is hidden within, and how the supernatural is expressed in the natural. That is what counts. One cannot simply link some meaning by arbitrary statement acquired by simple habituation with an exterior fabric. This would be allegory, but not symbol. Indeed, we should not speak about knowledge and learning at all, but about a process of embodiment by which one experiences a symbol coming to be, the thing becoming a means of its own self-expression. Man must experience it as a possibility for the expression of his religious interiority; therefore, also as a sign by which he can perceive the interior state of the other standing before him.

THE INDIVIDUAL AND COMMUNITY

The carrier of the liturgical action is a human being who connects things in his spiritual self-expression. However, this is not sufficient: the human being as a whole person has to take up the whole of creation in his expression of himself. Where is this nature of the human being? Where man is linked to community—predominantly, in the supernatural; he is an individual in the community of the human race. Transposed into the religious context, this means that humankind may only be fully Christian where the Church and the individual person are linked in an essential reciprocal relationship.

God himself is wholeness. His self-revelation and self-communication are geared toward the completeness of mankind. The completeness of mankind is not primarily to be seen in nations and states; these have a different kind of sense. Its uniqueness, taken in itself, and evident as it is, the completeness of mankind is primarily manifest in the individual living person.

Further, it is visible in the genus of humanity, taken in its entirety. Both the individual-wholeness and the complete-wholeness are imbued with something super-temporal, super-historical, and necessary. The two realities are interrelated: the person occupies a place within the wide span of mankind's community; the community of man, insofar as it is formed by individuals, is carried and finalized by them. There are two ways of reaching the completeness of mankind starting from the individual. In the first way, all intermediate links are skipped: family, nation, state. This is man's immediate attitude. By the second way, the individual encounters the wholeness of every independent link in and through the family, the nation, and the people. There will be times, circumstances, and special dispositions whereupon the first way will be appropriate. However, they seem to remain the exception. As a rule, this way is false and inorganic. By seeing the individual from this perspective, one tends to avoid recognizing the particular realities of circumstance and place in which God has placed him and in which he has to prove himself. One withdraws from the specific to the general, indeed into the noncommittal. Whoever seeks to make sense of mankind in this way will find it only as an abstract concept or as an object of hazy understanding. Crisp clarity in form is lacking, as is the task in which fidelity and creative power can prove themselves. Absent is embodied reality; a reality that would confront him with very specific demands. In this way, the individual may evade his position in history and take refuge in a lack of history since the actually historical lies neither with the individual nor with mankind as a whole. Both are embedded in their super-historicity while the actually historical rather abides somewhere in between. The real and actual place of history is the nation, the state, and the individual only insofar as he enters into a people or state. The event of history is constituted there: in the situation in which the individual is placed, together with his duties, his responsibility, and his fate. In the community of a nation, the individual encounters humankind as a whole. Not humankind as such, but humankind qualified by a specific nation. Only in his nation does humankind become concrete to him. He sees the nation as humankind's living link, distinct, charged with its proper task and its own fate. He stands in relation to the whole of humanity but lives as an extension of the enrichment of his relation to his own nation and state.

Therein lies the *organic* way of mankind—which differs from the *mechanical*, which puts nation and state aside to look only at the immediate whole. The latter denies concrete responsibilities rooted in a nation and in a people, as well as historical co-responsibility, leaving the individual to gain all too easily an undetermined and noncommittal attitude devoid of duty and responsibility. This is the *internationalism* that appears in either emotional or doctrinal masks. It is contrary to every nationalism and attitude, which sees only one's own world of nation or state and assumes everyone else as an inimical other to be preyed on or exploited. The attitude we are speaking about, on the other hand, roots deeply in the essence of one's own nation and state, and embraces mankind as a whole. This attitude includes a striving for the universal community of man, yet it only becomes embodied in a given historical context.

The same is true for the Church. In her exists a *universalism*, which is directed at herself as a whole and at something general; when dealing with individual tasks in the diocese or parish she always withdraws herself into her universality. This would be a history-less attitude, which would be either rationalistic-doctrinal or romantic-emotional, fruitless in either case. Certainly, we have to want the Church as a whole, not least because she was founded by Christ in history and stays united with him in it, but furthermore because she has a wholly different embodiment than natural mankind does.[40] We are supposed to say yes to her, love her, live and work in her where she appears to us in her immediacy: in the diocese, in the parish. There is *Church* for us. It is not separate, not even somewhat autonomous; but the Church is what it means for us to be in a parish, our position in a diocese, and thus organically expanded and linked into the Church as a whole.

God is turned toward this living wholeness of man. If we want to answer God, we must approach him from this same state. The wholeness of human nature must be in an expressive relation to that about which we have spoken. Liturgy is the religious action of mankind reborn. In it, the Church faces God, and at the same time, she faces the individual, if this individual is a member of the Church. The Church and individual encounter one another in the concrete parish community with its historically

---

40. It remains a question if a living, united humanity is even thinkable without a Church. More on this subject below.

particularized relations and duties. The Christian community of human beings, the Church, prays, sacrifices, and renews itself in the liturgy; the individual lives in his community, as he lives in the community of the Church. The Christian community was founded on Pentecost when the Holy Spirit descended and his message—the salvific message of Christ— became intelligible from the mouths of her apostles. This community came to conscious life twice: in the first centuries of Christianity and in the Middle Ages. In Christian antiquity, the call to "teach all nations" resounded clearly. St. Paul's great notion of the body of Christ with its many members was alive in the expression "There is neither Jew nor Greek, there is neither slave nor free person, there is not male and female; for you are all one in Christ Jesus" (Gal 3:28). This disposition was stabilized through the unity of the Roman world empire and the all-encompassing Hellenistic culture. During the Migration Period [*Völkerwanderung*] this early sense of Christian community suffocated to arise anew in the Middle Ages. Once more a political unity—that of the *Holy Roman Empire*—was present, at least as a conscious ideal. There was again unity in education, enabling students to begin their studies in Bologna, continue in Cologne, and finish in Paris or Oxford. Yet again culture enjoyed a unity, which fostered the fullness of ideas, words, and forms of expression filled with social, artistic, societal, and spiritual values in relation to the attitudes of a previous time. There was even a unity of language: the Latin of theology and jurisprudence was alive, spoken, and thought in.

All of this served as the basis for a deeper and more all-encompassing unity—namely, the Church. The Middle Ages had a concept of individuality. Stronger and more original personalities lived in the Middle Ages than in the ages to come. Their self-awareness was yet not critically sharpened; they did not retain their individuality at the cost of the community, but were integrated within it as something given. Tensions in politics, economics, and spirituality were common, as well as deep religious contradictions. But all were embraced by a communal-Christian unity and affected it from within to enrich it and imbue with new life. Modernity aided self-awareness to sharpen itself critically, and separated itself from the objective relations, yes; it even took the contrary position to them. Nations understood themselves ever less as parts of an encompassing whole, of Christianity. The great community of spirit, language, and forms of expression—in a word, culture—fell into partial unities. Each one developed on its own, understood itself as an independent fullness, and contradicted all the others. The one lost its natural connectedness with the other, the instinctive responsibility for it, and the capacity to unite with the other to form a higher unity. The capacity to be a member was lost; what developed instead was the isolation of modern man whose new *nature* was not connected with the rest, and did not want to be connected—at least he did not think that he would want to be. Moreover, concomitantly, the great community dissolved in the historic succession of the centuries: tradition was lost. All became a mere *today*.[41] With it disappeared what can be called *school*: the continual pursuance of questions through centuries, living-through and forming-through to the furthest depths. Its place was taken by mere creating out of the simple now with powerful optimism, reckless experimentation, and the dull refusal of everything received from a previous time and personality.[42]

A new development has already established long-time roots. It began on two sides. On the one hand, man relearned how to see what is real and to see the reality of another man. He learned to understand himself as a fellow man and to feel responsibility toward the other. From this, he comes to feel a great, all-encompassing unity. The sense of a nation seems to undergo a transformation. This new sense seems to differ from the old consciousness of a nation as a new individualistic feeling seems to differ from the old personality: personality and nation will shed the individualistic. Person and nation will surely and unquestionably assert themselves, but will also be able to find a place within the great whole. Thus, the consciousness of occidental unity seems to arise anew within nations. It is

---

41. To be more precise, there is no real today. The restless drive of modern man is alien to a standing in the fulfilled present since he does nothing more than deny his yesterday and foster in the hasty tomorrow.

42. I must repeat. When we demonstrate here that the Middle Ages were superior to Modernity, our words have no Romantic undertones. I mean neither that Modernity is bad and without proper value; nor do I demand that our time should emulate the Middle Ages because it was the universal *Catholic* time. Both would be wrong, the latter even heretical. Every time has its mission and value in one field at the cost of missing out in another field. Every time should and can be Christian, and should always remain—despite its particularities—within the context of the whole. Finally, every responsible person has a duty to stand in his own time, neither to flee backwards into an idealized past, nor to flee forward into a utopian future. But I wish that—as for example, Paul L. Landsberg had in mind in his book—the Middle Ages make us aware of what we lack, make us aware of what education means, what community means. Not as to imitate it! Rather, so that we may get a feel for real and fake again, for young and old. And so that in the Middle Ages, or if necessary, in contrast to it, we can find our own form of being. "History should not make us smarter for another time, but wise forever," I believe Ranke said. Not imitation, but self-reflection and self-discovery is intended here.

within souls themselves that the will to a European community of spirit seems to come alive. The will to life seems to broaden itself, unsatisfied with an exclusive community limited only to one's nation. It demands a higher grade of liveliness; it yearns for community with a wider spectrum and a wider sphere of influence. New situations arise that demand responsibility, new tasks of politically moral work. Values become visible that hitherto had not been seen. A higher and wider degree of will to community and consciousness to community was precious to the youth movement, which, in this aspect, painfully separated itself from some of the *old ones*. This is very different from the empty mixing of nationalism and internationalism.[43] The central idea consists of a community of spiritual and political-economic life in which each nation maintains its uniqueness and can be assured of doing so—yes, only so will it fully become itself because *being a people* means to have a mission toward the higher whole. Only as a series of unities will the nation become what it is called to become according to its essence, just as a hand that only when it is together with the foot and the heart is a hand, the hand of a body. The idea of a European life- and fate-community, having endured certain historical events, begins to take form.[44] Above all a concept of mankind takes shape. Many currents are united in it: economic interests are closely linked, political areas of action grow into one another so that a closed field forms, cultures enter an ever-growing intensive exchange. This conception is also spoiled, like the one of the European community. It needs to be purified before it can be made useful again. We do not speak of one homogenized culture, a mixture of nations, or a denial of one's own history, or some uprooted way separated from one's country and history. The concept of mankind is indeed organic and true to reality. Individual cultures in which peoples are known to be connected must be strong and free in themselves, on their own account. They have to become carriers of a mission for mankind as a

---

43. It would not be difficult to show how *Nationalism* and *Internationalism* enable one another in general. Approaching from opposite directions, both destroy solidarity between people, the forceful manifestation of the individual, and the respective relation of all in one which nature and Christianity demand.

44. MCV note: See Romano Guardini, "Europe—Reality and Task," in *Caring for Man* (Würzburg, 1966), 253ff. It also appears in a later edition, Romano Guardini, *Caring for Man*, vol. 1 (Mainz: Paderborn, 1988), 238ff. This is a speech that the author gave on occasion of receiving the *Praemium Erasmianum*. In it, he shows how effective the idea of Europe has developed in constant discussion with historical-concrete reality.

whole, the final link for a unity encompassing the whole of humanity. Those are all the vertical layers.

The horizontal layers are somewhat different. First, we must address those layers related to one's occupation. In one's occupation the multitude of possibilities of the individuals working together form a unity in the end. They rest on a basic value of culture (science, art, health, jurisprudence) and are supported by a certain image of human perfection (the occupational archetype of the doctor, the engineer, etc., together with his respective human and moral values). At the same time, they relate to the whole in a way that occupation reflects how the individual is linked to the community. A man's job is his cultural-sociological place-to-be. If he is a link in the political-social relation within the community and relation to the state, he equally becomes a cultural link through his occupation. His occupation creates societal status, which works like a cross-section: vertical layers of the political community. Within it, special values and images become living characteristics of his kind; they communicate to their carrier the solidarity of interests and the feeling of responsibility.[45]

All of that—a new capacity to live in community with one's neighbor, to see super-personal unities, to find one's place within them, to grasp and synthesize whatever is below into higher levels, and thereby form them into a construct of living members—all of this will bring to our period in history that which is similar to what the Middle Ages enjoyed in their own right: the capacity to live within the extremity of two poles, the individual and the super-imposed divine order.

This development will also confront the countries of Europe and North America with the decision, which we have already, to strengthen religious perspectives, which possess the original power to synthesize the autonomous-human and the Christian.

The Catholic Christian and the autonomous humanist may both confront the idea and the task of forming a community of nations with their respective spiritual attitudes that we are speaking about here.[46] This "and"

---

45. In many other fields, too, we can observe the same will that wants to order organically the chaos of individual appearances. This intuition detects certain things and events which share a common essence and causality as *image*. By way of this *image*, a person sees related groups of appearances—not in themselves, but in general and essentially related to one another and to the whole. Herein lies the contemporary way of thinking according to types, structures, morphological laws, etc.

46. Another question obviously remains, whether the Catholic Christians truly do this if they use the powers given to them—if they truly are and live as Christians.

is truly purely theoretical because the way of the first has a place in the global Church, and the other remains in itself and divinizes autonomous humanity. The latter therefore poses the wrong conclusion although he initiated the task of investigation with the right disposition appropriate to the topics. This disposition primarily consists of the power of objective community building—something proper to him. This means the capacity to expand the closed-off personal world into a greater unity because the pre-given and objective super-personal already is contained in him and leads him beyond his individual self. This power originates in the natural connection of the tribe or in the pagan state of modernity, which makes a totalitarian claim for power—which can obviously be something destructive. Yet the Catholic Christian who has similar powers faces the same task, but he knows how to order them within a unity with the higher supernatural. He turns this power into a tool of grace so that he can achieve what would not be possible to construct with merely inner-worldly powers: the unity of humanity.[47]

Maybe what has been said involuntarily reveals a confession, which is that the Catholic is at bottom *pagan*; that is, that which is truly Christian is missing in him; that he *super elevates* the fundamentally pagan into a Christian attitude of soul. However, these attacks repeated a thousand-fold still remain false. The Catholic attitude connects the essential Christian attitude of standing under the cross with the devotion to grace, and the letting-it-be of all creation with the *one* will of God, which retains a positive affirmation of all reality. All of this becomes merely human when one separates it from the *cross*. Oh, how much has the *essence and appearance* of Catholic Christendom been misunderstood! Surely, it itself laid out the occasion after it was cornered into a counter-reformatory attitude. This will disappear[48] because its inner premises have vanished. It remains to hope that Catholicism will become fully sovereign once more, living purely out of the wholeness of its own essence, within a unity of unbroken Christianity, which embraces all of nature unabridged in itself.

---

47. Their unity in general, not just religious unity. Out of the general relation of nature and grace there seems to come a natural unity of civilization and culture of mankind, possible only by religious power, something impossible by merely *natural* powers—as impotent as the former may seem today.

48. MGV note: This was said in 1923. The place of a post-reformatory hardness has been taken by more ecumenical openness, a promising novelty for the unity of Christianity though it also has the danger of sacrificing the strictness and clarity of truth.

The Church will rejuvenate herself. Consciousness of her will receive a new width, might, and fullness.[49] She will become conscious of the embodiment of what she really is. She is the Christian *whole*. She is not *home*—such would correspond to the vision of a person who needs support, the desire of one who, exhausted by the pursuit of the ideal, dwells in a romantic image of the past. But is the infinite cosmos *home*!? No, she is fullness, the *kingdom of God* on its pilgrimage into becoming, borderless and endless, standing underneath the cross. She deals with the fullness of all Christian content and forms: Christian life, realized in a multitude of degrees, ages, and fates; in all its social levels, national customs, and cultural groups. Above all, she is the essential connection between the super-terrestrial kingdom of the renewed heaven and those who are being purified within her. The reality of the Church embraces the complete fullness of Christianity, which unfolds in history because she embraces the fullness of all that is human that is directed toward God. This image of the Church wants to enlarge the consciousness of each person in a new way and to unlock new possibilities of living with, of participation, and of being responsible. All of history is included within this unity, tradition as the fullness of events as they find their sense in the "kingdom of God." For the Catholic Christian, the past is alive in his presence, and he knows that his life and actions will carry into the future. A certain palpable serenity springs forth from this, which is rooted in history and eternity equally, and which is open for the present moment but yet also freed of its violent clutches.[50]

---

49. MGV note: If we are not mistaken, then this presupposition has come to term in the charismatic personality of Pope John XXIII and the Second Vatican Council.

50. This does not mean that in the Church all values that have been produced in any place are stored next to and on top of each other. It should not be thought of as a large, fixed system in which everything is put in its category. Neither should the little *Catholic person* be thought of as one in whom all attitudes, convictions, and forces were combined and balanced against each other. This *human* would be paralyzed, could not live; but that is not the Church of history. Just as a special peculiarity always emerges in the living human being, so in the living Church too the special powers and truths emerge that are needed at just the right time. What is Catholic about it is that the relationship to the whole remains; her inner openness and immensity. It is Catholic because the individual does not fall under the spell of his peculiarity, and the Church does not succumb to that of the historical situation.

MGV note: Maybe the latter is especially worth emphasizing today after the Second Vatican Council for the theological self-understanding of the Church. [Translator's note: See especially, Romano Guardini, "The Church of the Lord," in *The Meaning of the Church* (Providence, RI: Cluny Media, 2018).]

The Church and her individual members carry the liturgy. Truly liturgical action is only possible with a wakeful consciousness that is filled with sentiment toward the Church. It dilutes as soon as the Church dissolves into individualism or when she narrows her mission to ethical-pedagogical constructs with another purpose. Equally inadequate is a vision of the Church merely as an organization of faithful, a kind of spiritual nation. From failings as these, the Church in the post-reformatory time withered in her understanding, which had previously been alive. During the medieval period, the concept of the Church contained a part concerned with law and organization. But in the foreground was the all-encompassing religious unity of life, the mystical community of those reborn in God together with Christ and their relations among one another. These truths led to the formation of two concepts: the *Corpus mysticum* and the institution formed by her hierarchical order. The former roots in the thought of St. Paul (especially the letters to the Ephesians and the Colossians) and contains in a nutshell the words of Christ himself—remember the "farewell speech" in the Gospel of John.[51] Accordingly, all those reborn in the beatified Christ are one with Him, as limbs are one with the body. The two facets of the supernatural principle of the life of humanity reborn are the image and power of man, raising individuals into a larger unity of life, just as the soul is unified with the body. Every limb of this grand construct has its place of effectiveness within a larger whole and thereby serves the other limbs and is carried by them in turn.

The second concept rests on a Neo-Platonic thought.[52] According to it, all things are connected by an all-encompassing, infinitely branched out hierarchy of levels of rank and participation. Here this idea alludes to the mysterious and harmonious relationship within the sacred Trinity, which is expressed in the teaching of *circumincessio*,[53] the threefold sacred relation in which God's life unfolds. They seem dry concepts for us, but for the medieval man whose sense of order was refined to such an extent that we cannot hope to achieve, they echoed a sublimely harmonious melody. The

---

51. MGV note: See Guardini, *The Message of John* (Würzburg, 1962), 12ff.

52. MGV note: See Romano Guardini, *Systemic Elements in the Theology of St. Bonaventure* (Leyden: Werner Dettloff, 1964), 93ff., 143ff.

53. Translator's note: *Perichoresis* (from Greek: περιχώρησις) is a term referring to the relationships of the three persons of the triune God (Father, Son, and Holy Spirit) to one another. It was rendered into Latin as *circumincessio*.

same is true for the choirs of angels, which number three times three, each one mirroring the divine relationships. The same laws also apply to the order of the Church with her three times three hierarchical levels of offices, ranks, and degrees. Each step mirrors the one higher and acts as the channel mediating the flow of light and love from the Son of God in an always more profound way. The *Corpus mysticum* and hierarchy are expressions of the same fundamental concept, according to which all living things come from the Father, through Christ, by the power of the Holy Spirit and are reborn in a world of the deepest community of life, rich, strong, and full of clear order. The pre-Tridentine era meditated about this mystery of the Church. Then the concept of canon law moved further into the foreground, the idea of an *ordered society*, the *societas perfecta*. However, in the ecclesiastical fullness of being, this concept embraces only the external aspect and actually possesses little religious fruitfulness. It represents the strongest powers of the political and the juridical dimensions, discipline and fidelity in relation to the kingdom of God, but it offers no real nourishment for the deeper religious powers. As long as it reigns, the consciousness of the Church lacks the living element, which carries liturgical action. But indications are on the rise, suggesting a reawakening of the temporarily dismissed line of concepts that had been pushed to the background as well as the feeling of life that belongs to them.

This Church: the infinite community of life in the *Corpus mysticum* and the all-embracing structure of order with its hierarchy, freely strengthened by the formal edifice of canon law—the whole not a static, immovable system, but living within the historical hour, forming it and receiving from it—that is the "I" of the liturgy. And every individual prays liturgically if his consciousness awakens to this concept and he joins himself within the ecclesiastical unity of the Church.

But the Church is given as a living thing within the diocese and in the parish. It is not a noncommittal construction of the world, but a living body, which is given for us exactly there, where we are: in the parish community and its special relations, tasks, needs, beauty, and poverty.

Therein lies yet another task for liturgical education: formation requires a religious consciousness of community. A faithful member must broaden his religious consciousness continuously, his prayer-self. He must overcome individualistic segregation and sentimental-romantic subjectivity so as to place himself fully in prayer, sacrifice, and sacramental action within the great community of the Church—the Church and not a "circle" of the likeminded. Not in the Church in general, but in his parish community. This community may be bitter, at times plain, and even cold. But his sense will be reopened again to see the nobility and strength of this attitude, nobler and stronger than all pious lyricisms and romantic particularities.

Such a broadening of consciousness must be achieved. The individual must make himself fully independent of whether he *feels community* or not. The experience [Erlebnis] is not central, but the individual must acquire discipline and a conscientious attitude. What he fulfills are not sentiments of the convent, but the knowledge of the world-ranging totality of the Church and the will to stand within it. His sense of self must be enlarged to encompass the community-self up to the point where the great "we" is the subject and center of prayer and sacrifice. Self-interest must be broadened until it has learned to take upon itself the content of the lives of others, their worries regarding salvation, their suffering, and their intentions.

An aspect of this discipline[54] will be the initiative of placing the individual into the living community of those present around him. He will widen his sense of self and his self-referentiality to the *circumstances* of all those around him. In connection with this task is the act of overcoming the aristocratic-esoteric shyness of the masses, exaggerated sensitivities, blunt senses, as well as spiritual sloth. The *we* must be realized in a living fashion: I and this person to my left and to my right; the old man in front of me and the woman seated there with a face full of worries, those standing by indifferently, etc. One has to engage on the level of the individual in order to really overcome any resistance and to give the *we* concrete content; there is no other way to escape one's own individualistic attitude. Then one will be able to enter the community: the sick, all those who could not participate, those who did not want to, those in special relations and grievances, each with his own needs and tasks. One will then unite parish communities within the dioceses and unite oneself with the bishop who leads

---

54. In all exercise lies the danger that it may become lifeless, formal, and artificial. However, exercise belongs to every true growth. It does not come about by itself and not by experience alone. Much must be worked for and exercised. Here we do not want to speak of *methods* but only realize what the core essence is.

them. This exercise will culminate in the encompassing of the Church worldwide.

Church-consciousness must be unfolded with care. In prayer, the person must think of all the different countries, parts of the world, and cultures as they are united in the Church. He thinks of the cultures and nations that are still—or again—alien to the Church, and he approaches them. In his spirit he will unite himself with the great number of those joined in one fate: the poor, the sick, the inconsolable, the searching, the fighting, the dying. He will remember the different levels of the Church—lay people, priests, bishops, the pope—and unite himself with all of these. He will remember the mission of the Church that is the annunciation of the Word of God in the tumultuous circumstances of the world, the Church's charitable work, *caritas*, and the spiritual life. He will also address some especially urgent hardship of the Church, a special task, a grievance, an error, a scandal, an omission, and will carry it before God. Finally, he will unite the Church on earth with the larger all uniting One and Holy. He will think of those who are still in the process of purification and will pray for them. He will turn toward the infinite realm of light and rise up to the beatified and will declare with them the eternal "Holy, Holy, Holy."

Consciousness is widened through this sort of discipline. It will be filled with living content, so that it may not remain empty. He will also be preserved from dissolving into the homogeny of the masses, since his cares will be filled with immediate and specific content.

This is an arduous task demanded of him and of everyone, especially those who are more individualistically minded. It is therefore necessary that we do not let ourselves drift away in the creative spontaneity of religious sentiment—no one who knows how rotten our state of soul really is will deny how much a truly spiritual-interior life rests upon pious discipline and how much religious sloth, sentimentality, and spiritual licentiousness often hide behind the refusal of such discipline.

In such work, consciousness of the self awakens, which in the liturgy speaks to the infinite God.

THE OBJECTIVE

All that we have written up to this point in seeking to understand the liturgical attitude has taken expression as the point of departure. This perspective alone could lead to a dreadful end, should it be falsely understood to imply that the liturgy dissolves into the subjective. Now we must again turn our attention to and attentively analyze the objective. From this point of departure, the liturgical attitude of expression will achieve its full meaning by integrating itself into the fullness of all relations of being. This is even more evident as we remember that the objective is not added extraneously to a subjective event of expression, but rather arises out of this event and its essence.

Expression can be understood in two different ways.[55] It can be understood as merely subjective. Then it means the revelation of something proper, such as an experience, a personal infatuation. In this sense it is self-expression. More precisely, it is the expression of that which is only actually meaningful for the person expressing it. It may be significant for those related to that person as well; but as for the rest, they will remain indifferent; for them it remains a mere fact. Self-expression as revelation of the subjective-individual may in itself not even make the claim of being significant for another. It cannot want to be more than a purposeless outpouring of the self, of one's own joyful or sorrowful life, a pure way of being-there. It retains a meaning for the one expressing and for God to whose honor it is expressed, in the same way as one may dance for the glory of God. In addition, self-expression cannot claim to be anything other than a gift of love and trust to those people who are dear and close to oneself. In this way it could form community but only from one self to another *self*—taken as a mere standing-in-oneself—and only between those two; a coming together into an extended subjectivity.[56]

---

55. To see the inner structure of this relationship, it has to be dissolved into types—types that are aids to reasonable thought. In living reality, these types flow seamlessly into one another. The concrete form is always the unity of contraries and cannot be thought of categorically, but can only be seen live and realized with creative work.

56. The author knows how questionable the thought can become that in itself is correct. Whosoever does not want to lose himself in the tangle of threats in which living things are woven must—at first—use some force. And that person may do so, if he is also ready to reintegrate whatever he has taken out of its context back into the whole, where it belongs.

But if a man aspires for his self-expression to have greater meaning for another, by growing out of either a life source or a living form—which could be a cause of joy to others, perhaps even a little bit of wisdom—though that would go too far—if one were to intend for his personal experience, though his own through and through, to have meaning for another, then by this he would demonstrate an unbearable pretentiousness.

Certainly, something else is possible, and the possibility is already opened by the aforementioned. Pure self-expression, an expression of mere experience, could have objective value for all others: namely in those human beings, pure in essence, in whom the subjective would become archetypal [urbildlich] for others, or in those whose fate has been so interiorized that others could draw from it as from a true revelation of wisdom. This is possible, and has indeed happened. The term *canonical human being* [quintessential human being] has been coined to indicate this sort of person and is particularly applicable to numerous saints.[57] Every human being can potentially profit from their example. However, this kind of commitment should neither be sought after, nor even be imagined. It has to arise on its own and autonomously. To demand it would immediately be presumptuous and laughable at the same time. It would endanger those who are treading their own path by tempting them to change direction and be lured into a lifestyle that does not fit them. Nevertheless, upon closer inspection we recognize that within the possibility of the merely subjective, another order arises, opening up another direction of meaning, veering into the opposite direction. Something arises and is born thereof, centered and originated elsewhere: the essentially objective. Let us leave the borderline cases on the side for now and return to a real trope of univocal subjectivity.

Once a subjective attitude has been radically developed, the object of experience itself becomes marginal; only the experience itself, the sensation, the event, and the condition that the object provokes become essential.[58] The state of experience is of importance here, but not its objective content.

---

57. Translator's note: Sts. Francis of Assisi, Benedict, and Ignatius of Loyola come to mind. Adam and Christ would be *canonical*, since they represent all that human nature has to offer (each in his own way).

58. The religious formula is very telling for this approach: not what, but that one believes, is essential. The same could be shown for all dimensions of life.

This means that violence is done toward the object, be it due to a lyrical or an expressionistic disposition, or whatever else lies at the core.

The subjective itself will be just as much in the way, as will be how things are drawn into this relation of expression. The proper determination of their own essence-image, inner rhythm, the particularity of their material, etc., take a step into the background. All are reduced to a trigger of experience, sensation, and material for expression.

Community becomes similarly subjective. What would be community is reduced to the extended self, rather than toward persons ordered toward a whole, toward a unified society with its own inner essential image and inner causes, something the self would have to acknowledge. The environment becomes a mere echo that embellishes the self, a means of having an alleviated experience and a larger expression of self. This type of community—as much as a thing of experience—is completely noncommittal in itself. It collapses when the feeling that seems to support it collapses.

This attitude toward expression is challenged by another figure of speech. In this other expression, experience is imbued with greater strength and a deeper profundity. It does not rest on experience as such, but on the content of the experienced: the object itself holds the weight of the expression. It is not feelings, emotions, and states which seek to be expressed, but realities, truths, and essences. The self wants to convey the things. Through its own reality, it is related to real external things and wants to reveal their hidden natures. For the self-aware person who fits into the first trope, the world of things will lose its reality, since he loses his reality; at best it will become undetermined, in need of form. The world dissolves easily into a stream of states and perceptions. At that level is the center of experience; around it and above it swirl waves of perceptions, forms, shapes, which trigger experiences and perceptions. In the second trope, one feels oneself a reality among realities and unmistakably perceives one's own proper sense of self. Its experience is seized by meaningful self-possessed essences, demands, and relations. If the self wants to express its experience, it does not do so under the special hue of *how*, but in the content-oriented definitiveness of the *what*. Its passion is geared toward this, that which retains something better, something hard, beyond its splendor. This self also wants to reveal itself, again as a what. To reveal not what it feels, but what it is. Not its experience, but its essence. It wants to reveal its proper being, which does not get caught up in experience, but preexists experience—that something which in its substance is independent of the ways in which it is experienced. Therefore, the term *self-expression* assumes a completely different sense. It refers not to the self-revelation of the spiritual life, which would posit the subjective as its proper essentiality, but to the expression of the self as a super-subjective being, objectively given reality that is and acts, indifferent to how it senses itself. The first attitude described here remains caught within the current of experience; it is this-worldly in the truest sense of the term. The second is other-worldly and oriented toward eternity; it is rooted in the metaphysical, in what is lasting, in the necessary. All doing and speaking receives another type of severity, univocity,[59] and tranquility. The great line appears, a strong, simple form, and with it, clarity and self-evidence.

This self-revelation happens within the depth of being, obedient toward its inner image-character. The self reveals not *how it feels*—which always remains non-committal—but what it is: objective self-expression. This demands a clear view, attentive listening, and obedience. Subjective self-expression demands that the person express sensations, the inner workings of the original resonance of a momentary feeling; objective self-expression demands a descent into essence, beyond the waves of emotion. The definitive core lies within in its fine individuation of being unique, as it is only in this moment, presently unfolding; here lies that which lasts: the root of being.

In this type of approach looms what was described above as the bordering potentiality of subjective approach. That which on the level of the individual is essential and lasting; that which needs to be expressed has meaning for all. If a man is so essential that his subjective experience—with all its originality—also becomes characteristic in this way, then all must be eager to see not just what, but also how, such a person lives, to learn wisdom from him and to follow him.

Our interpretation of this attitude can be sharpened: we can differentiate between what is essential and what is *merely there*. That which has

---

59. Translator's note: *Univocity* is a philosophical term denoting that there is a single meaning of a word (opposed to equivocal—multiple meanings of a word). I think RG says that man must "practice what he preaches" and not try to say one thing and do another. One could potentially say "authenticity," or "genuine," as well.

a right to be stands in contrast with that which is merely actually there. A criticism born out of being arises from what it is supposed to be. A critique of what is merely given by the idea. Therefore *real* transforms into *essential*. The more essential, the more real. Thus the idea becomes more real than concrete reality; the canon participates more in reality than matter of a given shape. And this idea, this canon, becomes the measure of all.

If this archetype is left on its own, a relativization of the real will follow, but from another side: being is threatened by that which persists. If the attitude has reached this point, then it will see danger and dissent in all that is particular and fleeting. Then it will turn into stasis and all blossoming fullness will die, frozen by the cold metaphysics of essences. Life freezes over under mathematical law. It becomes coercion; what it loses is its right to that which it is supposed to be. The canon takes power over life.

Different means of expression are employed with this attitude. Language and the words by which it is composed have proper laws. The body has its laws, as does each of its limbs, each line, each movement, and each gesture. The objective will to expression does not perceive the body as formless material subject to the formative sovereignty of the expression of experience. Expression rather means the awe-filled acknowledgement of the proper law of the medium. This proper law must be seen within the higher law of that which needs to be revealed and serves the whole organically. To "express" means to express something higher in something lower. The lower something retains its proper nature; it is ordered and heightened. Objective expression is deeply natural and objective. It does not belong only to the essence expressing itself, but also to the proper law of the medium in which the expression is realized. The same is true for the things that are engaged in this way of expression. They are not misused; they are rather freed toward their own true essence. They serve the whole in such a way that they remain what they are. In addition, only by service do they become what they are meant to be.

Because God entrusted all things to the service of man, he gave man dominion over creation and assigned him to the task of arranging things into proper order. The same is true for relations between human beings. All other people are independent of my will and my sensations. I ought not to estrange them from their essence; I have to affirm them as they are in their own right and in their freedom. Community is a foundational order according to its own essence; it embraces all members without coercion or the destruction of the individual. I myself cannot create it; it exists within itself, and I have to take my place next to others. Community is not simply a circle of people around me as an expression of my essence, but is formed by the person who is willing to enter into it with others as they are, into an objective unity. Living in community does not mean selecting and forming other people, even just in thoughts, according to one's own wishes. Living in community rather means accepting others both in their bodily presence and in the reality in which they live; be there joy or need, one receives them, anyone who extends his idea of self to an idea of community consciousness. This attitude of expression also turns the community into a *greater self*, thus extending one's own possibilities of expression. Still, though, the community is not to be formed according to one's own image, as living in community must account for the proper content and laws of others and try to emulate them.

This naturally presupposes that there exists an objective community and a "preestablished harmony" between the inner side of man and his external form and movements of the body, between men and things, and also between individuals. The single empirical community must be constructed in such a way that this harmony can appear in the foreground.

These are the two poles and orientations of every manner of expression and therefore of all culture: one toward the subjective and the other toward the objective.[60]

The former is creative in the specific sense of the word. It springs forth from the current of life, takes the self as the glowing point of all experience and the means of expression as matter, which has to obey the will of expression fully and without any demand from its proper nature. Both object and matter are seen from the alternative perspective of this experiential core and given new meaning. The ultimate consideration that needs to be said here lies beyond the object of experience, even beyond inner feelings, as the innermost layer of enclosed meaning. The path toward the essential is not the object and its own proper nature, but the self-glorious experience. Things and their proper meanings are drawn into this process to serve as

---

60. There is yet a third that is in the proper sense personal and linked to the concrete. Within it there is no distinction between the objective and subjective—as explained above. This type we must lay aside for our present inquiry.

material for the self-magnifying will to express. In the community, this pole of expression manifests similarly: the expressing person draws, indeed forces, the community into a state in which it becomes an echo chamber for his will to express. He dissolves the community's resistance and proper nature, reorienting it toward himself and making it docile to establish it as the basis for the action of his self. The will to express is dominion—dominion over object, thing, matter, and community.

The latter attitude is service. In service, the self and its experience stand as the mediator between the objective essences which it expresses, the means of their expression according to their proper natures, and men in a true community. The objective content of one's proper being, the essential content of his object of experience, the proper nature of the matter of expression in the body, thing, and community—this is the attitude. The subjective experience as such is but one level upon which essences manifest together in a concrete and unified life.

Up to this point, we have distinguished these attitudes from one another. However, throughout our reflections it has become clear that they can in reality only be together, with and next to one another. The essence of the concrete is to persist in contrary powers and structures. The concrete fact of the living expressive attitude can only be objective and subjective together, dominion and service at the same time. Only the ratio in which these two attitudes balance with one another changes. The nature of the self-expression, be it of the individual, the culture, or any special order of the spirit, is determined by which of these two weighs heavier. And obviously other factors contribute as well—for example, in the expressions of ecclesiastical life within the Christian experience, in general.

We would repeat something that has been said many times before, if we set out how the objective attitude has been loosened since the Renaissance and the Reformation. Compared to its contrary, the subjective gained power in a conscious or, at least, factual event. Evaluations shifted; the place of the medieval objective *order* as measure and image of right being and action was overtaken by the self-glorified individual in his subjectivity. The objective was dissolved entirely, no longer understood as a real order of a self-standing world of things, but only as the logical structure of the world of consciousness, the *absolute subjective* [subjekts überhaupt]. The accent of the world-view, the spiritual focal point drifted into the subjective. For a time both attitudes still remained related, such that they could shape a culture full of the force of life and power of form. The Renaissance and Baroque accented the subjective but had the necessary objective underpinnings to embody an image of the essence and a style reflecting a certain unity and grandeur. The shift of this fundamental constituency continued, slowly overstepping the borders of the inner fullness of being and the life of the individual within the whole—that is, the conditions of culture in general. The individualistic-subjective attitude came to the forefront.

However, even here we can now see a turnabout. Objective values[61] and an attitude ordered toward them surface once more. Let us think of the meaningful advance toward the object in the sense of the object, or phenomenological objectivity, as expressed in phenomenological philosophy; let us think of books such as *Metaphysics of Cognition* by Nicolai Hartmann. In the artistic fields, in social, political, economic life—everywhere a decisive conversion from the individualistic-subjective to the integral-objective attitude is announcing itself.[62] We stand on the threshold of two cultural eras. What is first at stake is that the objective attitude will gain some semblance of prestige beside the overpowering subjective attitude. The first step will be a sort of hovering equilibrium to be followed by a certain tipping over toward the prevalence of the absolute objective.[63]

How the youth movement has developed is telling in itself. What announced its beginning, the renunciation of the old in favor of authenticity, derived from an elemental experience of being-the-other[64] and from the feeling of life, which felt itself out of place in the old—where everything was merely *subjective* in the first instance. It became something like the final culmination of the subjective attitude. In the manifesto *Hohen Meißner* (1913) every basic experience is formulated from the spirit of

---

61. All values belong to it, which are related to continuity, tradition, balance, and unity.

62. See, Romano Guardini, *The Meaning of Church* [Providence, RI: Cluney Media, 2018], chapter 1.

63. Of course, this is not to say anything about how the upcoming culture will develop. Least of all, I think, will it be a kind of *return to the Middle Ages*. The positive impact of time on the individual and his subjectivity must remain undiminished. We have to create a new objectivity as people who have gone through post-medieval and modern times.

64. Translator's note: The *other* is a philosophical concept meaning the "opposite person or thing." In this context, RG seems to say that the Youth Movement was not looking at themselves first (individualism, nationalism), but at the *other*, to practice *compassion* and to *experience* not oneself but other people.

Kantian autonomy. This was the highest culmination of subjectivism—yet, paradoxically, it was at the same time its overcoming.[65] The mere demand for *truthfulness* could have been subjective in and of itself. Soon it took on a wholly different sense. It transformed into the demand for *essentiality*, and with this word the truly new broke open. Whosoever truly experiences this and is serious about it will face reality in a truer inner relationship than before. He will see the objectivity of true reality anew, feel it, affirm it. He will stand among real things as a true essence. He will not be one to seek self-glorious experience, but to experience being. Even in the language of the manifesto, which sounds Kantian, the words may have a different sense; behind them lurks a different kind of attitude than Kant intended. This human being lives according to his own meaning, not in the Kantian world of experiences. He instead lives elementally with a true soul, in a true body, with given things. He stands together with particular persons, ordered within the real world, surrounded by the only objective order of being and things, and finally in relation to God who is the origin of all super-essential reality. He knows that the laws of thought and the laws of duty are in their core laws of being. He senses that it is his duty to build his life out of reality and essentiality, not on concept and mere experience. Essential attitude: for the one who does not speak it, but who understands it according to its original sense, this word contains the culmination of the *new*. Becoming the true essence of the soul, of the body, of man, demands it, as does the essence of things and the community. God demands it, who revealed himself in the incarnation of Christ—and that is what it is all about. No more *experience* as the ultimately true attitude, but *seeing*. No more feeling, but *listening* (attentively) and *obeying* [horchen and gehorchen]. No more giving rise to an unspoken novelty out of one's own self-glorious originality, but acting and working obediently according to the objective order of reality. Discipline is an essential feature of all of this. Discipline builds life and being out of the essential laws of reality and places them into objective order. This basic will acts, often still unconscious toward itself, seeking bodily being, essential ways of living together, and forms of education and schooling that do not drill but *form*—that is, help the hidden-living to come to its essential image, which in turn forms its form [Gestalt].

---

65. See Romano Guardini, "On the Meaning of Obedience," in *Auf dem Wege* (On the way), (Mainz, 1923).

This was the underlying rhythm of the youth movement and the will of the *Hohen Meißner*. Here the movement gained new vitality. In the will toward truthfulness it freed itself from old ossified things and then from itself. It internalized that the deepest sense of liveliness is not arbitrariness, but discipline. Being in truth and reality replaced the romanticism of experience and feeling in the central place. Truthfulness does not mean that all that comes from within has a right to be. It means obedience toward true essence, one's own soul, things, the community, the world, and finally God who is Creator. Then truthfulness could mean standing up against one's own feelings, the arduous act of freeing the true core essence of all things from whatsoever covers it up. It can mean an action against one's own self, without any feeling. Then what "ought to be" and what will not be felt first can become alive and will be felt stronger as that which was subjective-spontaneous at first. In this way, truth is discipline, obedience, and service.

This is the great task that is given to us: to connect the originality of experience, the power of experience, and proper sentiment with discipline and obedience toward the objective. Should one go forward on his way with a carefree attitude toward reality, he may revel in the untested power of his youthfulness. But when he collides with reality, only then will it be decided if his youth is true and whether he will able to apply discipline to himself and to remain young within it, or if he will become a philistine like those against whom he had rebelled, just in a different way.

The sharpest contrast against the objective is evident within a historical perspective. There, where the reality of which we speak does not belong to nature, such as with the construction of soul or bodily life, but to a historical event such as a political situation, a certain state structure, or a historically proven fate. The subjective attitude denies the binding nature of history. It seeks to construct something new for the future out of momentary experience and overly historicized principles. This subjective will has its proper place and its actions in certain moments—such as epochal situations of change—that will form the future. But it has its limits. Its opposite is the objective attitude toward that which is concretely present: historical heritage, the developed forms of state and society, the historical situation, fate. Therein lies a great act of discipline: to stand firm and listen to the commands of reality as it reveals itself in a historical moment. The historical gives rise to the whole weight of the objective in positive law. In positive law, such as the laws of a state, subjective attitude sees something external, something non-committal. It is only binding by its own experience, by the conscience, which accepts a sense of autonomy, the meaning of this word which it gained by the most recent ethical developments. The objective attitude on the other hand sees something real that demands obedience in the rightful formation of a law; not obedience out of fear or because of an incapacity toward one's own action, and also not owing to the presence of a philistine stagnancy,[66] but because there is a strong will to discipline, to reality. Thus, it is at last a will toward new culture, new tradition, and new fidelity.

All of this is beginning to stir in the youth.

What has been demonstrated up to this point is also applicable in the religious sector. Serious liturgy is that form of religious behavior in which the objective is the strongest to manifest. Its opposite is the subjective attitude that carries one's personal religious immersion, the expression of one's own experience, special dispositions, needs, and fates. Between these extremes extends a fluid transition, including the great number of ordered religious exercises that have long since been formed by tradition itself, individual and folklorist devotions, and so forth.

The liturgical postures of prayer are forms and expressions tied to the objective state of the soul in the body—expressions of what is human in things, expressions of the individual in a community. All in all they reveal an objective attitude in which the subjective desires, feelings, and experiences step back behind reality and essence. It does not aim at self-glorious formation, but selfless service.

Here religious action is also expression, but taken from the objective perspective. It is not that anything at all is to be expressed, rather that the right thing must be expressed—that is, the true essence of man. The right attitude, not arbitrarily appearing, but as it is supposed to be. Instead of expressing every feeling that comes to the surface, only the right and objective feelings that are worthy of being pronounced in the face of God ought to be expressed.

---

66. Herman Hefele emphatically explains this attitude in his book *The Law of Form* (1919). What he tried to expound on a large scale was not the most precious, most true, and *most Catholic* at all, since the latter also embraces subjective and realized energies. It would be wrong to equate his attitude with the classic Roman-Catholic outlook.

However, how does man become true to his essence? How does he achieve the right mindset, feel the right thing? When he is asked for an image to model his formation, his answer ought to be "the way, the truth, and the life" (Jn 14:6)—that is, Christ. Since Christ is the essence of all essences, the eternal image according to which "all things were made" (Jn 1:3), it is to the extent that the human being is "formed according to Christ," and as much as Christ is expressed in him, that he becomes true to his essence. The essence of the created human being only awakens to clarity when he enters his living archetype and allows himself to be formed within it, allows his scattered-ness to be ordered, the wrong expelled, the imprisoned freed, and the right relation reestablished.

Liturgy is the self-expression of man, but of man as he is supposed to be. Thus, it becomes a severe discipline for him. The man who remains on the surface of liturgical prayer may find it easy and *unessential*, but the one who realizes himself in liturgy is the deep, essential human being. But his being lies submerged. Therefore, liturgical prayer must be a conscientious exercise until the deep and essential awakens, one's image of being is put in the right place, and the essential can truly speak. This necessary liturgical *re-becoming* [um-werden] has been rarely seen. It extends deep into the human soul; values have to be ordered completely differently, something totally other must be perceived as beautiful, and something else as ugly; man's whole disposition has to be reformed. Another state of consciousness, another order of values, and another way of feeling is demanded of him. It is no coincidence that this started to take off during the liturgical renewal. The movement demanded pure sense as an attitude of soul, in deep accordance with the will of our times. Liturgy is the self-expression of man. However, it tells him: a man who you are not yet. You have to go to school. You have to become the man who you have to be. Until then, your truthfulness must be one of obedience and discipline, and not one of spontaneous sentiment. As much as you become the man you are supposed to be, Christ and the Church will ensure that you may not be *deformed*, but reach your true self. He who redeemed you is the one who fills the Church, and his Spirit forms the liturgy. In the measure in which you become this man, your truthfulness will become one with this original sentiment.

This content is not expressed in the arbitrary, but in essential words and gestures. It is true that these gestures lack the unrefined freshness of the novel sentiment that grows out of expression; yet compared to those, they seem to be fully tranquil. The originality of the sentiment is not rejected, but it belongs in the realm of subjective-affirmative action. While the liturgy acknowledges and even presupposes this, the liturgy itself wants something else. It draws out the true essence of the content and the timeless essences of the means of expression: words and gestures of the body. Whatever is expressed in the liturgy is essential; expression serves the essence of the dialogue between God and soul. How the liturgy reveals these is also essential, and how it, in turn, serves the essence of body, gesture, and language.

The youth[67] are beginning to grasp the meaning of expression anew and are learning to distinguish between the subjective and the objective, between how expression rules and how it serves. Youth grasp anew what it means for expression to be at the service of the mystery of God and the soul; a serving obedience also toward the essential image of the word, toward the inner sense of the movement in kneeling, standing, and processing, in the shape of the hand and posture of the body. The form of expression thereby becomes free with respect to its internal power and beauty. All of this happens in the liturgy.[68] Word and movement are fully formed. The posture of the hands, the manner of bowing the body, the gestures of the different liturgical performances, all of these are strictly stylized. Nothing is abandoned to spontaneous inner movement and sentiment. Everything is choreographed according to the laws of an attentive sense for form. The depths of the words, which are rhythmically formed, only reveal themselves to the person slowly. Yet ultimately, all remains *natural*. How does the standing one *stand*! How is liturgical walking really *processing*! How revealing is the essence of the hand, the most ensouled of all organs in the attitudes and gestures of the holy service! How

---

67. MGV note: Much of what the Youth Movement had rediscovered and introduced by experiment has already passed on to general praxis, especially in the field of education. Accordingly, the law that the Church repeats in the fields of culture and spirit thirty or forty years later in the post-conciliar reforms received a proper place in the praxis of the Church.

68. It should not be overlooked that some texts of the liturgy are schematic, others are purely rhetorical and have little content. How could it be otherwise in such a giant work, the creation of which took a millennium and whose texts fill the heavy volumes of *Missale, Pontificale, Rituale,* and *Breviary*! But that is why the *Ordinarium Missae* in its severe majesty is filled with many orations of transparent clarity, powerful formulas for the administering of the sacraments, the responses of Matins with their interweaving lines full of wealth and benevolence, and many other things that are true masterpieces.

simultaneously powerful and simple are the—good—liturgical texts! The priest who pronounces them countless times throughout the year knows that were they different, he would grow weary of them. The celebration of the Eucharist remains ever new, ever unique.

It is no different when things are drawn in to this relation of expression. They carry their essence in themselves and become part of the liturgical expression according to their essence. We must dedicate a special moment to parsing out how much the things are grasped and formed in the liturgy. They are not participating, so to speak, in a naturalistic or raw state; rather they are *super-formed*, *stylized*, in the liturgy, as liturgy is an expression of culture and not of natural religion. This is evident by many individual features. There is always a right measure for things: bread, wine, salt, fire, water, oil . . . ; form and action always remain very simple . . . , always submissive to the word; never does the force of nature overpower the spiritual sense.[69] The matter is always elevated into more meaningful being [Gestalt], as is realized in the bread of the host or in the blessing and anointing by the sign of the cross. Much more could be said about this truth. Naturally given resources are always reshaped by *culture*; yet their essences still reveal themselves. Bread remains simple bread, fire remains flame, glow, and light. No violence is done to the thing as to coerce it to express something untrue to its nature. Quite the contrary, its essence is liberated. In the liturgy, all things take up heightened self-evidence, as it was in the old folklorist customs, which had grown out of a particular context of life. What happens here is *service* toward the creation of God in order to redeem and elevate natural things.

What is true for body and thing also holds true for the community. In the book *The Spirit of the Liturgy*, I tried to explain the essence of the liturgical community.[70] True community is service toward humanity. This kind of service demands that the individual be considerate toward the other, to acknowledge his autonomy, to insert himself into a common order, even when he has to put his own wishes and desires last. It means that he truly and internally takes the life and opinions of the other onto

---

69. Let us remember the difference between liturgical baptism and baptism in a stream of water, the liturgical blessing of water in the Easter Vigil and the blessing of St. John's fire!

70. See Guardini, "The Fellowship of the Liturgy," in *The Spirit of the Liturgy* (San Francisco: Ignatius Press, 2018).

himself, while at the same time he keeps himself at a proper distance. Our time is passing from an individualistic yesterday into a collective tomorrow—both are equally distant from true community. One needs to have conscientious education to understand what essential liturgical community truly is.

The objective resonates with a sharp contrast in the liturgy since the individual stands opposite to the positively historical condition. The liturgy is not designed theoretically, but historically. Therefore, it contains many idiosyncrasies and imbalances, just as a human being who has undergone much personal development, or a people have trodden a long historical path. There are also manifold shortcomings.[71] In the liturgy, the history of two millennia and multiple cultures becomes present; the individual in his own present must acknowledge this and must try to live in it, as much as they strive to emphasize their own judgments on these things. And the liturgy is positively put. It is not metaphysically necessary; its basic essential features are done positively. They could be different, too. The Church decided upon much of the liturgy. It could be different, but it is what it is. And as it is, it holds true as long as the positive law of the Church will uphold it as true.

All of this poses a difficult challenge for the rebellious spirit of the individual who likes to be the measure of all things. He has to step out of his limited narrow position of having conquered a small part of reality in the here and now in his short life, by which he wants to judge the infinities and duration, depths, and essences. It is truly a hard trial that the urgency of the present should be silenced in the face of the heritage of the past, and that the proper will of the individual stands silent before the authority that is placed there. History and law, tradition and authority—these embody the objective with proper force and put the personal attitude of the individual before a difficult trial.

All of this must be carried by trust in the Church.

---

[71]. Anyone who advocates the liturgy is also obliged to speak of its shortcomings. And everyone who tries to get serious about it knows that it has quite a few of them. The texts of the psalms are good examples, such as the readings of Matins, more precisely the readings of the second and third Nocturn. Also, the extent to which the breviary has a monastic rhythm—that is, it expects a daily schedule that is not available to those living in the world; and other examples of this kind. None of these are short-lived complaints, but long-felt and often pronounced deficiencies.

This trust can see humanity reborn in her, the basic concept in which Christ and creation enter into relation with God. He sees in it a true organ of the Holy Spirit and believes that Christ possesses the *might of the word* (Acts 6:4). He sees her being, life, and action become expressions of what is the essential Christian. This trust gives him the possibility to place the thoughts, judgments, and sentiments of the individual into the background, and at the same time to recognize the consolation that the soul can find its true self in its self-abandonment. The Holy Spirit has imprinted his seal upon our souls and transformed our bodies into his temple; he knows our essence better than we ourselves know it. The forms of expression that he teaches us are deeply formative. We should grow into them, even if they do not correspond to our sentiments, and at first, they do not seem to us to be "truthful." They are truthful because they are essential and thusly belong to a deeper level of understanding. Let us live in them, and we will become free toward our true essence—then is and ought to will fall into one. Then we will have the "freedom of the children of God" (Rom 8:21). The *law of prayer* is also the "perfect law of freedom" (Jas 1:25).

Herein lie new tasks for liturgical formation: we must step out of our subjective narrowness and arbitrariness into objective width and order, and we must kindle joy through the determination toward obedience and strict discipline that lead to such an attitude. The Church alone can guide us down that path. Therefore, we must overcome all misgivings toward her and instead take hold of a deep trust in her.

We will not be able to enter into practical suggestions; here we are speaking mostly about the proper attitude. Through his self-abandonment, man must change his attitude of remaining-the-self and adopt an attitude of finding himself. That he wants to remain right, that he measures everything by his own limited being, that he confuses the voice of his conscience with the desires of psychological self-affirmation while also confusing the demands of the divine laws with those of his self-will—these must be overcome through obedient service. Weak religious life bloated with its lyricisms and sentimentalities, and with a passion for small pleasantries, must be overcome as well. The will to greatly form must awaken anew, especially in religious life. The judgment that a great and objectively ordered life is *empty* must be recognized as a spiritual weakness, which has the strength only to revive small things, bound to lose its breath before great forms and wide orders. A small spirit can handle a lyrical poem or an intimate novel. But Dante's gigantic edifice, *The Divine Comedy*, itself is a world full of life that cannot simply be read but in which one must submerse oneself in order to understand, because we need a power of soul, which we still lack. It will certainly not be self-taught. However, it would be philistine to recognize only that which falls within the capacity of one's own measure and limited power. It appears to us that there are sectors and attitudes of life that lay far beyond lyrical intimacy and epic tranquility. The path toward them is one of discipline—hard, strict discipline; obedience toward the master and his work, toward tradition; obedience toward what speaks from eternity. Therefrom man can grow beyond himself until he comes to see all things great.

All of this can be applied to the religious sector. That someone may prefer a private devotion to the bitter coolness of the office of Mass shall not be taken from him. But he may never say that the liturgy is lifeless and static simply because he himself has not been able to overcome its wide and strong forms within his own soul. The man of the past would admit honest self-deficiency; the man of today would betray pedantic hubris. We must understand how deeply we truly are stuck in individualism and subjectivism, how starved is the drive for greatness, and how small the measure of our religious life really is. A sense for greatness in the style of prayer—the will to the existential—must be reawakened in prayer. Discipline and the abandonment of weak sentimentality may be achieved through earnest prayer; yet in this endeavor, one must adopt the resolution to maintain seriousness and obedience toward the work of the Church in one's religious being and action.

Therefore, it is necessary to prepare the soul for the grandeur of the world of the liturgy, and the magnificence of its attitude and forms. We should not just affirm this, but we should show it and reveal it! When the severe power of formation is felt in the individual, then the pure soul that demands a larger measure will answer. Let the joy that lies in discipline be experienced. Discipline is cool and cautious, but it has an inner glow. Discipline is power that can culminate in the highest tension. The same is true for fidelity to the Church. A sense for the existence of a higher mysterious order, once submerged in obscurity, is awakened. We will once again be capable of investing great trust in a power of life, which really extends into the depths of the soul; a power that has the courage to say, "this way and no other." We must develop an affirmative relation to the Church, to her institutions and her laws; we must trust her wholeheartedly.[72] We should not hold on to an idealized image of a religious community, measure the Church according to it, and then presume to want to reform her according to that image. The Church is the community that Christ wanted; she retains this identity in her historically-concrete, living being. We should distinguish between essence and appearance in her—but that is wholly different from distinguishing between idea and reality. We cannot and should not distinguish true essence from real appearance. Much of appearance may not be in accordance with her true essential core. This we see, especially since we love the Church, and we want to do our part, so that the external may become as the internal. We ought to begin by doing this where the first demand for true reform lies: in ourselves. This should always be sustained by the great affirmation of the whole living, real Church by both fidelity to her and love for her. From this perspective liturgical formation is ecclesiastical thinking, wanting, and feeling; and these can become truly a *sentire cum ecclesia*.

ON THE RELATION OF RELIGION AND CULTURE

Truth compels me to point out the deep problem in the thought processes of these attempts. I hope to achieve as a result that no one assess them as too high or in a faulty manner—also, if possible, so that my attempts are not discarded as something too unsophisticated.

Whosoever is faced with something alive must know that he can enact different things with the same word. This is first because a given thought can bring about very different outcomes, even harm or misuse, depending on its circumstance and inner constitution. Second, every living movement of thought or will seeks to go beyond itself. It could remain one-sided: it takes specific occasions, needs, and wants and aims at a specific result. Concrete life is not that one-sided; rather it shows a structure

---

72. MGV note: See especially Romano Guardini, "The Church of the Lord," in *The Meaning of the Church* [Providence, RI: Cluney Media, 2018].

of contraries. Every clearly formulated point of departure contains the danger of intruding into the wholeness of life to try to enforce, with unilateral severity, one thought with the consequence that it destroy the organically grown whole's inner measure and equilibrium.

In the sequence of our considerations, we have pointed out repeatedly the point where thoughts begin to become false, and we have restored their proper measure. Nevertheless, I want to repeat with severity the limits and dangers of our approach.

I want to retort very briefly to the criticism that here an inopportune, fashionable trend is inserted into the sacred realm of supernatural religion and the latter thereby put in jeopardy. This argument actually at least deserves an answer; it is equally the most comfortable to bring up, since it requires the smallest amount of exertion and understanding. At the same time, this argument gives whomever formulates it the appearance of being far removed from the problem, as if standing in the pure supernaturalism of faith. Yet one can be sure of a quick and broad reaction to this argument.

As easy as it is to make this accusation, so hard it is to answer it properly. Whosoever makes this reproach does not recognize the difference between what is eternal and what simply has been before. That is, the time since the moment in which that which now *has been* was itself new and seen as a *modernization* and *a novelty*. Here one can simply respond that the attitude that limits God's kingdom by something temporally bound and removes it from whatever is new and living is as un-Catholic as a restless striving for reform. That God has given the special mission of his kingdom's unfolding to every era should be reason enough neither to inhibit its unfolding nor to allow it to fall into excess or unilateral error. In our time, we also bear the responsibility of a special mission—indeed oft repeated through the ages—to staunchly defend the truth despite temptations of doubt derived from distortions and misled aspirations. It has always been a task for Catholic Christian spirituality to transmit what is true and live in time *with the Cross* so that the truth may be purified, balanced, and integrated into the kingdom of God. Moreover, what is today understood in these thoughts as *new* is in truth ancient. It is only new for those who consider the customs of the last decades or centuries something *old*. They forget that especially in this "old" thing, an earlier and precious heritage is abandoned. The same is true, I hope, with what this essay contains. New? In truth, it is ancient! Every page of the *Pontificale* and the *Missale* speaks to the person who reads it. Here, the soul frustrated with the inadequacies of time looks upon the ancient Catholic good and says, this is what I have sought.

Certainly, we as Christians have to be ready to live in contradiction to the times, and in some way the Christian will be a contradiction himself. Should we not rejoice in whatever time is given to us—this encounter with whatever may be proper to that time that is arising and connected with our ancient Church?

This could be another reproach: the search for the essential may be good. The idea-content of the faith can be grasped in its depth. In addition, a word and an image are meaningful customs that deserve to be nurtured. But all of these must be immediately translatable into life; that is, they must have a direct tangible, moral, and religious purpose. In the work for liturgical renewal this purpose is veiled—by the logic of this reproach, it is thus ultimately a waste of time and energy. This immediate criticism would also suggest that the spirit and form of this exercise must be immediately relatable; but the liturgy has an *antiquated* character. Further, it must be true regarding religious influences that the desires of the *average person* are taken as a measure, but not—as the liturgical movement has it—those of the small, even academic, elitist class. In a few words, what counts is the immediate, practical impact.

This way of thinking reaches deep into the way in which religious and pedagogical work is understood in general. The decisive question is: Should a formator aim for quick, tangible *successes* or should formation focus on essential virtues by which—maybe later but progressively and increasingly—individual effects will be realized? Should the measure be the momentary situation characterized by particular and specific needs or should it be what is eternal and steady? Should the basis of formation be the fulfillment of immediate understanding or should it be that which is precious? Average or excellent? Does formative work aim at short-term or lasting success? Doing or being?[73] As soon as the question is posed thusly, the answer is clear: a simple either-or does not suffice. Such a choice will

---

73. MGV note: See Guardini, *The Spirit of the Liturgy*, especially the chapters "Liturgy as Game," "The Seriousness of the Liturgy," and "The Primacy of the Logos over Ethos."

only be presented by the one who does not bear responsibility for others. It is always true that one must recognize spur-of-the-moment needs in one's work, since we always have to help, always have to *save*. But whosoever has to save cannot waste any time. It is continuously tantamount to address the needs of a given time, even those trends and fashions that are the most superficial, since many can only be reached on this very shallow level, and the pastor's responsibility extends over all those within his flock. It will always hold true that one has to work for the average; after all, to a large extent, daily life and reality naturally consist in *averageness*. But we should not forget the danger of this demand. It is precisely this attitude that made direct work with people—call it schooling or formation, be it social or religious education—so unfruitful. Organizations were established instead of lives; superficiality came to reign in place of depth. Symptoms were cured, but the root of the sickness remained untouched. This way of thinking makes continuously unassuming demands on people, and has therefore lowered the bar of life bit by bit. One experiences momentary success from following simple demands, while allowing fundamental demands to languish, leftover and forgotten. This has fashioned mediocrity everywhere; in truth, the average itself was lowered. Further, it has discouraged those who strive for excellence. The realm of religious culture has been forced to suffer a loss of greatness and strength.

Once again, we must learn to desire not the façade of success, but enduring core value; not quick and transitory action, but persistent being. Truly creative work, which creates by drawing from an essence, may seem purposeless, but in truth, it is saturated with purpose. This statement does not deny folkloric devotion the rights to exist. The authors of the "Way of the Cross" and any genuine booklet about the Rosary are safe from this kind of reproach. However, the hour is past to engage in education that reaches into the depths. In the religious realm, the liturgy is particularly crucial.

The reproaches do weigh heavily. They touch upon an aspect of religion that could be essential, at least in revealed religion.

Religion is not culture. In its pure essence, religion is the living personal relation of man with God. This means that God is affirmed to the fullest extent; he is given due *honor*; his *kingdom* is allowed to grow in and among people. Religion means that man finds the fullness of his life and salvation in God. The search for the meaning of life in God is religion, and it touches person after person. It is the most elemental part of life that exists, second only to hunger and self-defense, and awakens one's deep personal investment at the most critical moments: when life and honor are on the line. Religion is consciousness. It is my fate to be bound to God in all things to the last. And at the same time, in some mysterious sense, the fate of the reign of God depends on me. We must discern what it means for God and man to be tied together in such a relation. We may say this casually based on the assumption that there exists some kind of original relation coming from the teaching that man, God's creature, is created in his image. However, it is only true from one point of view. Fundamentally speaking, we cannot even name man and God with the same breath. We cannot even speak about them as two *beings* [Wesen]. Not even the *is* can be used univocally in the former case and the latter. Radical differences lie between the absolute God and the finitude of man. What can we deduce of the religious relation from this? It is unique and not comparable with any other. The religious relation is the most natural to exist, and it can grant perfect tranquility and perfect security.

Plainly put, man belongs to God with every fiber of his being because, "Thou hast made us for thyself, O Lord, and our heart is restless until it finds its rest in thee" (St. Augustine, *Confessions*). If we ponder this properly, the Christian relation will resonate with something of such extraordinary, unthinkable quality that we would feel it the most tense, even the most dangerous thing to exist—if our habits would rest from obscuring our thinking. We are dealing with a Being whose Being, Power, Counsel, Wisdom, Value, Purity, and Perfection, taken on their own account, exceed us in every measure. That should give religion the basis not of *fear and trembling* (Kierkegaard), but we should come to realize that we, each in our whole being, totter on a sword's edge, as we see in the lives of the great saints. Every human concept, every idea about what is great and good, every intuition about order and what befits us, every idea about what seems to be ordered and safe, is blasted by entering into the divine, by the personal and transcendent God. Every value must be questioned when God steps into the comparison. Even the whitest purity seems filth compared to the radiating purity of God. Every opinion about occupation or task, any work or accomplishment, seems to dwindle and gain an entirely different color and a whole different dimension of value when presented to God.

In addition: Man is a sinner. That fact in itself sharpens the contrast of religion's character beyond all measure. Man feels in his heart the "law of sin and death" (Rom 8:2). He remains ever unfit for God's demand. This additional incommensurability between God and man threatens our relation to the holy in an unparalleled and dangerous fashion: In and of ourselves, we are lost before God.

This is not the last word, however. Religious experience only receives its last and qualitatively proper character when we take into consideration the revelation of Jesus Christ. The sentence *Gratia supponit naturam* is true. Grace presupposes nature; but that cannot mean that Christ's grace is subordinate to nature. His grace remains sovereign and distinct from everything natural—that is, it remains supernatural. Christ's essence and call are not oriented by nature, but according to their own sovereign laws. They encounter nature, and nature has to obey. We grasp the meaning of this in the cross. The cross is the "stumbling block to the Jews and foolishness to the Gentiles" (1 Cor 1:23), for all of nature. It is the dissolution of nature's demands in the face of super-nature's demands. The dogma of grace, original sin, and redemption reveal the meaning of super-nature to us. It is the other side of religious experience. The sentences *Gratia supponit naturam* (Grace builds on nature) and *Gratia perficit naturam* (Grace perfects nature) each only touch upon one side of it. Together they form the whole. In the religious experience, the *supernatural God* (if we can call Him that) faces humanity. It is the Father of whom Christ speaks; it is the Holy Spirit who "blows where he wills" (Jn 3:8). It is the grace of Jesus Christ that reigns here—and gives ultimate tension to this relationship.

How many words of Christ and his apostles should be named here!—that it is "fearful to fall into the hands of the living God" (Heb 10:31), that we must "strive for our salvation" with "fear and trembling" (Phil 2:12), that we have to "wake and pray" because our "flesh is weak" so that we may not fall into "temptation" (Mt 26:41), that in every moment the Lord may return as "the thief in the night" (1 Thes 5:2), that God's counsel is essentially hidden "from the wise and learned" (Mt 11:25), that we should "let the dead bury the dead" (Mt 8:22) when Christ calls, that "man's enemies will be the members of his own household" (Mt 10:36), and so many others! All these come to one point: at any moment, God can call and throw into disarray even the most beautiful and profound order, even if the order seems decisive. At any moment, God's terrible purity may shine forth, and then we will see with trembling and unforgiving clarity our own guilt, and all inner-worldly cultural values will fade in its wake into something unessential. At any moment, God's infinite glory and sweetness may flow into the soul and bury whatever counts as precious on earth, be it action or possession, all will be as "rubbish." Thus it is. The life of every saint shows us this *reevaluation of all values*. Culture taken in its broadest sense departs from what is natural from the perspective of the value of earthly things, orders, and works; instead it seeks by continuous, cumulative work to emphasize what lies in nature and to construct everything in the realm of knowledge, art, societal order, jurisprudence, and economics.

Christendom and culture[74] relate to one another in this question. In addition, both comprehend why. Culture always strives to manifest itself as the essential and final answer, and to protect itself from the menace of religion. It either strives to devalue religion, reckoning it as necessary only for the brute and the stupid, expendable for the free of spirit who possess *art and science*; or it seeks to render religion innocuous, while simultaneously using its force by incorporating it and turning it into "culture" itself, in its last anointing. The Apollonian religion of the Greeks, Roman piety toward the state, the service of heaven in China, and all other forms of liberal and state religion have done this. Religion, wherever it has had life, has always retained itself in sharp contrast and with the hesitancy of mistrust for culture. At least in times of its original liveliness, religion seeks to keep culture at bay. We have to leave everything behind for Christ's sake. Earthly things are nothing before God. Earthly cleverness is like childish folly; yet the truth that real life only comes to be through the cross and suffering—something that counts as folly, ignominy, and failure before man—becomes that which is essential and lasting. Moreover, it is this truth that is quintessential for the living Christian. Thus, the practicing Christian's religious attitude lets him dismiss culture, as St. Francis of

---

74. MGV note: See Guardini, "Thoughts Regarding the Relationship of Christianity and Culture," in *Discernment of the Christian: Collected Studies* (Mainz, 1963), 145ff. In discussion with Sören Kierkegaard, the author seeks to address the incommensurable relation between *Christianity* and *Culture* seen from a Catholic viewpoint.

Assisi did it, or at least reduced it to a bare minimum in his own life. He eyes culture with distrust, seeing it as the great tempter. And with even greater distrust he views "religious culture"—that is, the fallacious attempt to unfold Christian reality by cultural means and to draw cultural norms into the religious sphere. This becomes evident in scientific dealings with truths of the faith, in religious art, in the unfolding of an ecclesiastical law, and in the jurisdictional dimension of the Church, carefully thought out religious education, and so forth. In all of this, the Christian detects compromises with the world, a deadening of the original tension. He detects the danger of God becoming too familiar to man; that man turns him into an innocuous figure, creating a barricade of things, words, and institutions before the possibility of experiencing the fundamental *decision*. A slow disintegration of the essentially religious may be felt therein. And here, ultimately, lies the deep admonition which can be brought against the liturgy. That is, it turns purely religious prayer, filled with all the tensions of the God-relation, with all the beatitude and trembling of a fulfilled relation to God, into "religious culture" whereby the pursuit of salvation and the necessary struggle with God kills the religious as such through its transformation into culture by pedagogy, dramaturgy, and art.

This is the sharpest reproach that can be brought against the thoughts laid out in the present pages as well. Here lies the *true danger* of the liturgy. Here lies the danger of all liturgical pedagogy—only for the person who does not understand it. That is why we want to explicate it with the sharpest clarity, sharper than truth itself, so that everyone may understand.

What is said here presupposes living faith. It presupposes that one be resolute in his pursuit of salvation and the kingdom of God. If one is not, then these pages are not for him. What is presented here seeks nothing but to be a means for true Christian credibility and service, and it requires serious and pious sensibilities.

If these are present, then goodness can spring forth. Even more, when there is goodness, then it is necessary.

In life, the pious man tends too easily to forget his need for culture. Mere culture may be superficial, discarding too easily the essential tension and seriousness of discernment; but the absolute release of tension leads, paradoxically, to a sense of dangerous and soul-crushing pressure. True culture gives religion the means to express itself, to embrace all of life, to create, and to form. It enables religion, as theology, to permeate the event and content of Revelation,[75] to form a system of laws and religious communities of the people of God as their *ordo*. As the source of liturgy, it can imbue prayer with the fullness of religious content and enrich it with every natural power in its fullness and manifoldness. Through moral teaching and education it can shape and guide life through its real circumstances and difficulties.

The Church puts to question every autonomous culture by her mere being. By her divine foundation, she has and always will do so. She is founded on the qualitative supernaturalism of grace and the event of redemption by the Incarnation and Crucifixion. She draws all hatred of self-righteous culture upon herself, from Celsus (a second-century Greek philosopher) and Julian (a Roman emperor from 361 to 363, also a philosopher and author in Greek) through the liberalism and positivistic materialism of our times. The continuity of the Church implies that she is always charged with the great responsibility of integrating the values of the present culture within a religious relationship. She is the intensive crux of religious culture. She has been reproached as the enemy of culture, the suppressor of culture; she has been accused of making Christianity innocuous, representing a mere manmade edifice of human ingenuity, power, and refined statecraft. Some have said that she destroys all the power and unity of nature with her supernatural goals; others have said she betrays God in his absolute claim to culture and veils his incommensurability, she cripples the momentum of the moment of decision with her casuistic approach. We say all this only to demonstrate that she is the Church; she is universal—she is truly *Catholic*.

The conscientious exercise of the liturgical life can turn into religious aestheticism. Should this happen, the Christian consciousness would be right to object, seeing the seriousness of the questions jeopardized, culminating with the question of salvation. In that case, the earnest but simpler folkloric devotion would be better than this kind of "religious culture."

It is similarly disastrous when unjustified distrust against the formation of a customarily religious culture arises. The consequences are dire.

---

75. Translator's note: True culture enables theology to permeate Revelation. I think what RG is saying here is that true culture (in the form of scientific theology in this case) enables religious sentiment to permeate the events (historical) and contents of Revelation.

The religious point of view shrinks, thought becomes superficial, and spiritual content as a whole suffers impoverishment. The life of the faith itself suffers.

Having pointed out all the *essential and necessary features* of liturgical formation, we see the necessities of due measure and understanding, "But these you should have done, without neglecting the others" (Mt 23:23).

CHAPTER THREE

The Liturgical Mystery

The first part of chapter 2 dealt with liturgical action. More precisely, with its empirical structure, the living human attitude that it carries, and the tasks education demands of it, all in keeping with its relation to the temporal whole. The result was that first and foremost the liturgical act is an act of man, of his living unity of body and soul. An attitude toward the symbolic grew out of this human basis, creating and receiving the expression of all the spiritual in the bodily, of the inner in the outer. In this fundamental relationship, all things appear nearby and the world as a whole appears to be drawn in by the power of symbolism and the embrace of spiritual, bodily expression, expanding and enriching. From there, we analyzed the carrier of the liturgical attitude, finding it not in the individual but in the formed community—that is, the Church. The individual is part of her as her member. Finally, we focused on one element which seemed to be of special interest: the objective. It became clear that we had understood liturgical action—the act of the expression of the spiritual in something material, of something internal in something external—too unilaterally. The activity does not exhaust itself in *expression*. Should it, then expression would remain only within and would be merely subjective. Rather, the act is built around two poles, the subject and the object. The objective communicates itself as standing in itself and as reality that measures the event of expression and demands to be heard, to be seen, and to be affirmed, and to be acted upon. Finally, in the conclusion of chapter 2, we pointed our attention to the fact that all that had been said can only be understood as a single moment within a greater whole. At first, we spoke of the empirical side of the liturgical act, its psychological and cultural-philosophical aspect, and the educational challenge that it poses. Yet those only make sense when seen from the religious aspect, the Christian reality of faith. Then we discussed the relationship between religion and culture—that is, between Christianity and natural-cultural reality. We discussed how these variables relate to one another in a peculiar antinomic way, challenging the other in one aspect while excusing it another. A meditation, such as ours, on the cultural side of liturgical action can only retain its meaning when this relation is understood with the correct tension.

Now we will continue with our inquiry, but in another direction. We will not take off from the empirical side of the liturgical act; but we will look at its religious content. The thoughts of chapter 2 have already helped us approach form and content. Now we want to focus on the core of liturgical action. We seek to find out what that core is. We will find that it is mystery.[1]

We cannot deduce the essence of the Christian mystery from historical, psychological, or philosophical presuppositions. What history has taught us about the construction of the mysterious and the religious is precious. It is also useful to consider the psychological inquiry of religious attitudes and events or the religious-philosophical inquiry of the essential phenomenon of religious mystery. All that remains is only an aid, neither the starting nor the end point. If we want to know what the essence of the Christian mystery is, then we ourselves have to ask. Since the Christian mystery deals with human personalities and communities, which bear the basic structure of human reality, some features of the religious-historical and religious-psychological, as well as of the religious-philosophical assessments, will be encountered along the path of our investigations. These receive their special character from the actual essence of the Christian mystery, which cannot be deduced from them, but can be demonstrated in its positive and unique *datum*.

Let us open the breviary to the time of Advent. There we will find the antiphons—short pieces of verse which pertain to the current period of the liturgical year or the special feast of the day, and consist of psalms— the foundation of the breviary as a whole. In these verses, which resound in the soul and hark back to the early morning prayers and Scripture readings of Matins, we read, "I see in the distance, see, the power of God is at hand . . . ; hasten toward it and say: Tell us, are you the one that ought to reign over Israel?" Or we read, "As the visions during the night

---

1. See both works of Odo Casel, OSB: "Das Gedächtnis des Herrn in der altchristlichen Liturgie" (The Commemoration of the Lord in Ancient Liturgy), and "Die Liturgie als Mysterienfeier" (Liturgy as Mystical Celebration) in *Ecclesia orans* II (Freiburg, 1920) and IX (Freiburg, 1922).

continued, I saw one coming in the clouds of heaven, the son of man . . . . " And, "I implore you, send, Lord, whomever you want to send, see the misery of your people, as you have foretold us, come and free us. . . . " So reads the whole text. Renewed once and again, sometimes confident, sometimes fearful, sometimes consoling, pleas that the Savior come. In the beginning, the expectation bespeaks great distance, as a prophet looking deep into the future to see the Messiah enter; then the anticipated moment feels closer and closer, until, just before the days of Christmas, we read, "Tomorrow, sin will be vanquished, the Savior of the world will rule over us." And on Christmas Day itself, "Today the day has dawned, the day of salvation. . . . "

Elsewhere in the liturgical year, in Holy Week, the liturgical texts express the event of Christ's passion. The Lord speaks, acts, and suffers, and the people pray as if they were present during this most holy event. "Our shepherd has gone home . . . today our Savior has demolished the gate of death and destroyed its lock." Slowly, the atmosphere morphs, until on Easter day the event of the resurrection appears in the texts. In the sequence of Easter, the question is posed: "Say, Mary, what have you seen on your way?" And the answer resounds: "Christ and the tomb of the living one, the glory I have seen in the resurrected one."

On the day of the ascension, an invitation follows in the *Invitatorium*: *Christum Dominum, ascendentem in coelos, venite adoremus!* The Lord speaks to his disciples, exhorts them, and bids farewell: "Do not let your hearts be troubled. You have faith in God; have faith also in me. And I will ask the Father, and he will give you another Advocate to be with you always, the Spirit of Truth. . . . " Then again, another time of expectation follows with the nine days before Pentecost when the disciples were gathered in the cenacle in hopeful prayer. The pleading call fills these days: "Lord of Glory, Lord of Hosts, you have risen victorious into the heavens: do not abandon us as orphans, but send the chosen one to us, the Spirit of Truth. . . . " Until, finally, the liturgy of Pentecost begins with the mighty *Veni creator spiritus*: "Come Creator Spirit," now, today . . . !

We could bring up countless more of these examples. When we examine liturgical events throughout the year, we see that they are characterized by the life of Christ. The liturgy has indeed no content other than the person, the life, the word, and the actions of the Lord. Advent is the first period of expectation. Christmas is his arrival. Until the day of the

Ascension, Christ's life occurs before us: his passion, death, and resurrection. Then the event of Pentecost follows, whereupon the Holy Spirit, the *Pneuma*, form and power of Christ, enters personally into the history of the world. And, finally, comes the time which Christian history understands to be the period of "all days until the end of time."

This whole order of times, prayers, and actions is focused on one historical event: the coming and life of Christ. But it is not merely a form of simple historical commemoration. What we are dealing with is not a *past* but a *present*. The temporal orientation of these thoughts, meditations, and religious acts, these events in word and symbol, do not return into the past, but manifest in the present: *today*. This does not mean that we are dealing with something super-historical or extra-historical, such as the idea of redemption or a religious myth. The liturgy is without a doubt tied to the historical person of Jesus of Nazareth and his work. His historical life is put into the present, not just in its content or its ideal meaning, and not just by way of the communal commemoration of historical events by persons who recognize their lasting religious content. Rather, the event itself becomes present and real.

This fact permeates the whole liturgy—here something transpires. That something is the life of the historical Jesus. Let us not grow tired of repetition. Let us see the problem with stark clarity. Not in the form of a living representation in the present, because a tension sets into the present an event which—in sober recognition—should be called something past. Not in the form of a dramatic representation, in which the actors and the audience know that what transpires belongs to the imagination and unreality, really lasting only in our memories. Also not in a pedagogical form of emphatic formation, which in language and sensible embodiment become the strongest possible experiences. These are all parts, but not what is essential. We can only grasp the *now*-ness of liturgical action when we personally enter into the realization of the liturgy and co-experience the event within a living community of the faithful.

How can that be? Of what nature is this *now*? How is it related to the historical past? What kind of event is it? In which form of reality does it happen, especially when in comparison to historical and imaginary reality, to the empirically concrete and imagined ideal actuality?

Let us pursue our inquiries by examining the most unique and lucid example in the liturgy: the celebration of the Eucharist.

The Eucharist is constructed of different parts. The first part is the Liturgy of the Word.[2] It consists of prayer, readings, and the homily, and ends with the Creed. The conclusion of the celebration is also wholly constructed on the Word. In between, we find the commemoration of our Lord, in which the prayers are related to that action which is about to begin. While most of the readings and prayers of the first part change depending on day and season, the prayers of the middle part always remain the same. The priest prepares bread and wine, and brings them before God. The Anaphora ends with the preface, the final words of which are the *thrice holy*, and the prayer of sacrifice. These are ancient texts, which in form and sequence go back to at least the fifth century, but their core is even older—the *Eucharistia*. Here we pray first for the whole Church, then for all who are present and their intentions. What follows is an act of unification with all the saints, a realization of the Christian community that spans above all times. "Our Lord Jesus Christ, the day before he suffered, took bread into his holy and venerable hands (while the priest takes the host placed on the altar), and with his eyes lifted up toward heaven unto thee, God, his almighty Father (the priest does so), giving thanks to thee (the priest bows his head), he blessed it (the priest makes the gestures of blessing), broke it and gave it to his disciples saying: take and eat ye all of this. (These words the priest speaks in a deep bow, then he genuflects, raises the host, lowers it, and places it on the altar.) For this is my body. In like manner, after he had supped, taking also this excellent chalice into his holy and venerable hands (the priest takes the chalice with wine before him), and giving thee thanks (he bows his head), he blessed (he does so), and gave to his disciples, saying, take and drink ye all of this. For this is the Chalice of my blood of the new and eternal Testament, the mystery of faith; which shall be shed for you and for many unto the remission of sins (the priest genuflects, then raises the chalice for all to see, and places it on the altar).

---

2. It should not be forgotten that the liturgical *word* is not only a means of communication between the speaker and the listener—a meaningful transposition from one logical and psychological subjectivity to the other—but is a living vessel of a holy, divine Spirit Word. The liturgical word itself has something of a sacramental character.

As often as ye do these things, ye shall do them in remembrance of me."[3] The text goes on: "Wherefore, O Lord, we thy servants, as also thy holy people, calling to mind the blessed Passion of the same Christ thy Son our Lord, and also his resurrection from the dead and his glorious Ascension into heaven: offer to thy supreme majesty from thine own gifts bestowed on us, a pure victim, a holy victim, an unblemished victim, the holy bread of eternal life, and the chalice of everlasting salvation."[4] This should suffice here. What does this woven fabric of words mean? What meaning does it have when we listen with an open inner disposition?

First, these words express more than thoughts. The first part of the solemn Mass consists of the communal reading of sections of Holy Scripture followed by a homily. As explained above, this part is therefore the Liturgy of the Word, of instruction, of prayer. After the Offertory and especially after the *Sanctus*, something else begins—action. Whereto does this action orient us? Action can be didactical. It can embody thoughts. Even in a dramatic fashion it can convey ideas. But this is not the case here. We are dealing with an event that rests in itself, not in order to achieve a certain instructional effect. We are not dealing with a certain technique for the development of the soul that is meant to awaken experiences and provide edification. The action happens in accordance with its own laws, indifferent to the pedagogical sense it conveys and the effects it instills in those participating in it.

This action is fully oriented toward a reality; an historical event. If we analyze the words and actions in a closer light, we recognize that it stands in an immediate relation to the event mentioned in Mark 14:22 and 25; Matthew 26:20–29; Luke 22:15–20; and 1 Corinthians 11:23–25. The account of Luke reads: "Then he took the bread, said the blessing, broke it, and gave it to them, saying, 'This is my body, which will be given for you; do this in memory of me.' And likewise the cup after they had eaten, saying, 'This cup is the new covenant in my blood, which will be shed for you.'" We see that the wording of the holy celebration of the Eucharist is essentially the same. Luke's text rests as its foundation, supplemented by additional prayers. The sentence, which only Luke and Paul, his teacher,

---

3. Translator's note: Translation taken from *The Daily Missal* (London: Baronius Press, 2019), originally published by Laverty & Sons, Leeds, 1960.

4. Ibid.

include, "Do this in memory of me," is adopted in its liturgical form from the First Letter to the Corinthians. While the text there applies to the chalice, "Do this as often as you drink it, in my memory," the text of Mass applies to the whole action. The text of the Letter to the Corinthians makes it clear that the Pauline sense of the text is intended, "For as often as you eat this bread and drink the cup, you proclaim the death of the Lord until he comes." The citation that does not derive from Scripture is the *Mystery of faith*. In substance, it does not change anything; yet we will see how significant it is. If we set all of this before our gaze, we will recognize that the action as a whole follows an historical event. It is the actual reality [Vergegenwärtigung] of an event, a "commemoration." With the words "Do this in memory of me," the sequence of primary action, that which we have been analyzing, comes to a close. The next begins with the words "Wherefore, O Lord, we thy servants, as also thy holy people, calling to mind the blessed Passion of the same Christ thy Son our Lord, and also his Resurrection from the dead and his glorious Ascension into heaven." Built into this *commemoration* is a longer prayer, which has been called *Eucharistia*, thanksgiving, since the earliest days of the Church. According to its concept, form, and some features of its content and character, it follows the logic of the liturgy of the Jewish feast of Passover. Indeed the historical event did first happen on the day of Passover and especially included the meal's thanksgiving prayers. In addition, it also continues the tradition of the Greek prayers called *eucharistai*, in which religious sentiments were formalized into scripted prayers.

This liturgical action presents itself as the memory of a historical event. But what kind of memory? There is a concrete action that has been called *actio*, or more specifically, *canon actionis*, since ancient times. This expression signifies the ancient Roman sacred name of a sacrificial action. Not only the words and thoughts, but also action and event. The priest's action itself is *commemorative*; it relates in a commemorative way to the action of Christ in the cenacle. It is not a dramatic representation of the event, but a realization of it. The way in which the liturgy is formed, the words the priest speaks, and the attitude of the community bespeak a commemorated and realized process. The sequence of the action is both commemorative in itself and identical to the event, which is commemorated by making the event real through the priest's actions. At first sight, this form of commemoration seems incomprehensible: a commemoration that places the content of the event into memory.

However, if we look with a sharp eye at the content of the commemoration, we will realize that that which occurred in the cenacle is not the only event being realized in this sacrificial action; indeed the liturgical action stands in living relation to the fundamental event of redemption: the sacrifice of Golgotha. The words of Christ himself indicate this: "This is my body, which is given up for you"; "This is the chalice of the new covenant, my blood, which is poured out for you. . . . " The relation is also evident in these words of St. Paul: "as often as you . . . drink the chalice, proclaim the death of the Lord." We have evidence of the Christian consciousness of the wholesale realization of the event of salvation within the Eucharistic celebration, which dates back to the earliest Christians. This conviction permeates the words of the Canon as we have it now and which can be critically demonstrated to have existed by the year 600—although, in fact, it is much older. It fulfills the whole liturgy of the Eucharist, which in its essential elements was finalized by the year 800. One prayer for the Ninth Sunday after Pentecost expresses the sense of this event: "As often as this event is made present, the work of our Savior is realized." Could anything be comparable?

Historical events belong to the past. Their uniqueness and unrepeatability belong to the essence of history, to its essence and to its dignity. Each event by a person to a person. History cannot and indeed should not be repeated. It stands before us with its own unique truth and value; and its uniqueness is also simultaneously its tragedy. In history, nothing can be redone. What has passed is past; what is lost is lost; what has spoiled is spoiled. Yet therein consists its wondrous safety: what happened in the right and good way is really so and remains unalterable. We are not dealing with the repetition of history. The thought that something past could happen again is unreasonable and indeed wrong. It would imply a historical doppelgänger; it would nullify the basis of our being. The personal-historical is wholly identical only with itself. It is unique in persons, unique in its process, unique in its social and temporal context: happening here and only here, now and only now. The claim of liturgical action is clear: it is not merely a psychological commemoration, symbolical representation, or dramatic representation. The past event resurrects itself in the liturgy.

History does not repeat. The same event really rises anew. The liturgical action becomes identical to the real event.

We would not hold it against anyone to say he finds this unreasonable and renounce any further explanation. Having said this, only when he does not make the claim to really know what Christian life is all about. If he, on the other hand, wants to do that, then such an opinion is unfounded. We are a religious community, which has consistently upheld our beliefs for almost two thousand years. We are not *primitive*; we are truly European. Are we composed just of ancient sentimental and fantastical thinkers? No, we also carry the highest cultural consciousness. Our past does not rest on a weak critical plane; rather it swells with a fully self-conscious reflection of a wholly historical development and the fruits thereof from a two thousand year period. Finally, our religious discipline stands blameless against the accusation that it is an arcane practice of bogging down spiritual inquiry using excuses about the historical, ideal, pedagogical, or subjective experience, for history shows our consistent public dismantling of such libel.

All of this demands a judgment. Herein stands a clearly delineated religious phenomenon that weighs heavily and has proven itself against the critiques of all thought and sentiment. How dense the imagination must be that presumes such a religious-psychological reality! Comparative religion shows that there are similar imaginations of this sort outside of Christianity.

Accordingly, a certain personality, a certain religious mystery in cultic form can be relived as something present. Let us think of ancient mystery cults, for example those of Orpheus or Demeter. Between these and the liturgical mystery, there are deep-seated differences: those celebrations are limited to relatively small circles and demand certain ethnic and historical conditions. The Christian event is essentially removed from these sorts of preconditions. It realizes itself in an open and free atmosphere of the soul full of specific tensions. It is independent of specific cultural, social, and historical circumstances, and claims its identity despite the changes and temporal succession of almost two millennia. It possesses an incomparably greater character of religious credibility, which—for the objective observer—weighs much heavier. Finally, all the pagan mysteries are based on myth. Even if the myths were at some point in time convincing, faith in Dionysius, whose life, supposing he lived on earth at some point, can be experienced in sacred rites, has vanished into thin air. Any critical thinker will understand that here we are dealing with myth: an event contained in the metaphysically representative and experientially religious. For the ancient, the historically real was charged with importance through its artistic form and metaphysically psychological experience; yet from our contemporary understanding of historical reality, we find the myth devoid of importance and easily thrown away.

However, the Christian mystery remains very strong in the modern relation to the historical-real. Christianity is history or does not exist at all. Progress in Christian consciousness does not entail dissolving it into history, the experiential, or the ideal, but the constant recognition of its deeper reality and resilience against questions raised from within. It belongs to the essence of the Christian mystery that it deals with both a historical Gestalt and an event. Despite all similarities to the pagan mythos in word and form, and despite all parallels in their objective structures and psychological realization, in Christianity we are faced with something that is incomparably unique. We come to the recognition that in the Christian life and consciousness, there is a peculiar phenomenon, a special form of event. On the one hand, it is the consciousness of a simple historical reality—of that which happens in the here and now: for example, that Jesus lived in a certain time, spoke and acted in a certain way. On the other hand, it is the consciousness of the realized event, that which is thought out, felt, and subjectively experienced—for example, the consideration of one event in the life of Jesus. Further, the Christian conscious remains free of the burden of change over time and fortified against criticism; it can rest peacefully in the identification of the event of Christ with the events of the liturgy and in the suitability of the external form of the cultic act with the person enacting it.

If we look closer, we will realize that here the relation, which governs the whole Christian attitude, becomes denser. How does the Christian stand in relation to Christ and his life? Here we come to the conscious recognition that he was as an historical fact. Then there is the meditation on Christ as the psychological operation in which both the person and life of Jesus become the object of thought, in an imaginary, thoughtful, and perceptive sphere. Then we encounter another relation in which the faithful stand before Christ alive today. Christ's person and life are not just something given, something real. They are not just the content of experience, not just objects of a pedagogical, didactical, or artistic realization. They are reality. It pertains to the essence of the faith-relation to Christ to understand that his life is not caught in moments of the historical past, but that it is present in today's reality. Today he is born anew; he lives and teaches; he addresses what he says to me today; today he dies, and today he resurrects. To come to Christ, I do not need to walk backwards down the way of historical memory. That I only have to do if I want to make an historical judgment about him, as when I see him like a figure such as Buddha, Mohammed, or Otto the Great. Yes, in that latter case, I would have to approach him like Mohammad or Otto the Great—that is, I would have to tread backwards through the testimonial knowledge about him from his day to my present. In the true relation of faith, I have a different relationship to Christ than to Otto the Great. In faith, I stand immediately before him. So that the tense particularity of this consciousness may not be deluded: faith does not mean to take something less seriously than historical knowledge; it is not an evaporation, not arbitrariness, not a pre-scientific or somewhat uncontrolled behavior. We should be way beyond such rationalisms. Belief is a basic act of our being which we cannot take seriously and strictly enough. When I say that I stand immediately before him in faith, the *immediately* is neither meant in a psychological sense as though I were imagining him, believing that he were present; nor does it imply that I take the figure of Jesus out of his own life and implement him into my historical reality. What it means is that it belongs to the basic structure of Christian consciousness that Christ be immediately present to every historical presence, objectively speaking. What we are dealing with here is not a religious-psychological fact, but a metaphysical-ontological fact: it is a problem of reality. We encounter the same phenomenon in the liturgical mystery.

When we analyze the meaning of the words of Christ, such as, "And behold, I am with you always, until the end of the age" (Mt 28:20)—when we analyze the meaning of the events of the Resurrection and Pentecost from this perspective—we recognize that Christ is present for the Apostles and for the young Christian community, not just as a past, historical personality who is remembered, but as someone continually present, with whom one can enter into an immediate religious relationship. The image of Christ in the young community and its relationship to him does not stand in contrast to the earlier and original images of the Gospel. On the contrary, another, equally essential part of the relation of faith steps into the foreground. Here, he does not just take a place within the remembrances of past events, nor as a figure hoped for at some future time; rather, he resides in the very specific consciousness of faithful in the present.[5] St. Paul emphasizes above all this side of the relation of faith to Christ. Separating Christian reality from false relationships to the Old Testament, thereby opening it to the whole world whom Christ addressed, was one task within salvation history, which belonged to him. In a potent manner, he brought it about that the living Christian faith knows itself to be in a loving relationship not just with the historical memory, but also with the present spirit of Christ. The former is not dogmatic-cultic dissolved into the latter, but is identical to it. This alone fulfills the content of the faith: a relation to Jesus Christ, the historically past and pneumatically present.

This immediate presence before Christ belongs to the essence of Christianity, to the essence of our faith relation, and to the realm of faith. As the end goal of the faith relation, one cannot merely leap forward to achieve it in a single bound. The first step lies in the first act of faith, indeed in the desire for faith and openness to it. The *imitation* of Christ is more than the remembrance of his example as it *was* in the *past*. It is a life with him and in Christ living *today*, in his present. The historical person of Christ, the Master, has not been replaced with the *Kyrios Christos* who demands imitation and adoration. The imitation of Christ presupposes a "being in Christ" (2 Cor 5:17; Eph 2:13) that is only possible after Christ's resurrection and transfiguration. Imitation is incomprehensible within sociological-psychological categories; it belongs to the ontological-religious models, which Sts. Paul and John coined: "Christ in me," "I in Christ" (Jn 6:56).

The immediate stance before Christ, this super-historical present being of the Savior and his life, fulfills the whole liturgical event. When we approach the liturgy with an open mind, we see that it is nothing more than a special form of the immediate relationship to the historical past and the super-historical present Savior. It is a special form since it is not rooted in the individual but in the community. It is realized not in the processes,

---

5. What is said from the historical-critical side in the *Kyrios-Christos* theory about this process does not affect its nature, but only its historical, psychological, and sociological mechanisms.

experiences, and duties of daily life, but in the content, events, and forms of the contemplative life, in the liturgy and in the cult. In the liturgy, the whole faithful community and the individuals within it stand in an immediate relationship to the Savior by essentially contemplative actions: contemplation, prayer, participation in the sacrifice, and sacrament. In this whole complex, the event of the Eucharistic celebration is the central core. Here our immediate relationship with the super-historical coexistence of the historically past Savior becomes present in a special way. The way is not a priori, but is taken from the liturgy itself; it is only possible as an effect of a divine act of institution and revelation.

Now we are approaching the innermost part of the liturgy: the fact of mystery. By this, I understand that in a specific, cultic-liturgical form, the real presence—not the historical duplication of the once historical Savior and his life—is brought in the present. This includes the claim that next to the historically-concrete and the psychologically-imagined being, another way of being becomes actualized.

Let us try to approach the life of the spirit of the present. When we examine how we approach space and time today, we discover a precarious double standard. On the one hand, we observe attempts to relativize space and time, more specifically, to subjectivize them by turning them into categories of the imagination of the thinking subject. Not arbitrary categories since these do not root in a random empirical subject, such as the inherited capacity to see colors, but in the *subject in general* [überhaupt], in the essence of *imagination in general* [überhaupt], therefore the structure of imagination as such. They nonetheless remain subjective, should one take this concept and apply it to its natural object: the thing [Gegenstand]. They are forms by which my imagination orders the chaos of sense data in a timely and special way. Alone, my immediate consciousness knows nothing of such creation of an object by the a priori forms of intuition. I know on the contrary—and that is the meaning of whatever is presented to me— that what is presented to me is imagined in the forms of time and space. Though I do not see things spatially, in fact they are. This basic consciousness allows me to affirm that every perception of space and time is a subjectification.

On the other hand, we encounter an absolutizing of space and time. Modern consciousness takes itself as absolute. At one and the same time, it does so with a mathematical-scientific-technical attitude as well as with an historical attitude. Technicism and historicism are compatible in that way. They take space and time as absolute. The former is convinced that things are absolutely spatial and can be grasped in a purely spatial-mathematical-technical way, that there is no non-spatial relation to them. The latter holds that things are purely chronological, that they can be approached only by way of time, and that a trans-timely relation to them is impossible. Epistemological space-time subjectivism belong together; they form the basis of the modern relation to the world, to things, to humanity, and to history. This relation seems to be in a state of change with another variation on the horizon. In it, things are seen as objectively-spatial and events as objectively-timely; the feature or being in space and time is not understood as absolute. The object lays not only extended in space; events are not just separated by time. The object cannot just be understood within a spatial *technic of relation*; the event is not just understandable by historical analysis. Next to the spatial mediation, there is another immediate relation to the things and next to the timely mediation there is another immediate relation to the events and to history.

The reader may be skeptical of the following thoughts. I will draw from the spiritual perception of time as an auxiliary construction to approach this special claim of the Christian mystery. My intention is to understand better how every living attitude that supports the mystery comes to be formed. I take from it a series of observations about changes in spiritual operations in relations between men, and the environment, and with the past. And I know of people who sense these things immediately and with great clarity.[6]

Our relation to that which is spiritually past and spatially distant is formed by a special type of mechanistic and historical-technical attitude. It originates in the determined distance between timely and spatially separate things. It focuses only on the way between events and sees things only in the spatial and timely mediation. However, there seems to be yet another possibility, a way rooted in the given reality of the present and the

---

6. As far as the basic idea itself is concerned, this is the intellectual property of Rudolf Schwarz, and I tread the same path he has. (See "Über Baukunst" [On Architectural Art], *Schildgenossen* IV, Year, H. 4, pp. 273ff.; also "On the Way to a New Historical Picture," *Schildgenoosen* IV, Year, H. 6, pp. 422ff.).

spatial-separate in the being-here object. There is a twofold way of imagining this: Either that I, alive now, could somehow reach back into that which happened in the past. Or that that which happened in the past could somehow be relived now in the immediately experienced present, itself the living substance of a human action. In short, the idea is that either I could reach from our present into that which lies in a distant past, or that something distantly past could reach forward and touch me.

We recognize that which we are speaking about. All that happens in time is also part of a super-timely sphere, all that happens in space is also part of a super-spatial dimension, and access to this sphere is possible—because all that has happened at some time could enter the living present; and all that lies somewhere in space can be present in every point of space. I would like to add that we consider this thought only in relation to the being and lives of humanity. This means that things and events do not happen in a form of space and time, but also stand beyond it in a different sort of dimension; there they are non-spatial and non-temporal altogether, all of them contemporary. This sphere is accessible under certain conditions from all timely presents and from all points in space.

Put another way, space is not the function of the next-to-another (mechanical space) but is the ordered in-one-another (living space); and time does not have the function of the one-after-another (mechanical time) but the ordered at-the-same-time (living time). There is an extensive and intensive space as well as an extensive and intensive time. In addition, neither function cancels each other out, but they actually presuppose one another. The living coordination of space and time—i.e., correlated coexistence and succession—differs from the mechanical atomistic relation, which lacks proportion. This all seems possible only when there is an internal ordering.

Once more, I emphasize: all of this is said only in relation to life. It is founded on the concept of the organism. This means that there is a living unity in a spatial *next* and a timely *after*, which affects its structural and functional parts (limbs and organs), as well as its chronological succession (steps of development). From the start, the parts of the living stand in and next to one another. In contrast to the mechanical structure, the essence of the organic begins with the fact that the building and affecting parts are spatially distant to one another, yet related. The plan that relates them is itself fully present in all parts of the organism, rather than commanded by an external ordering power with a blueprint in mind, as in the machine. The concept of the whole body, as a unity of structure and functionality, is present in the hand.[7] To be a hand is absolutely impossible without the body. This is true for each cell and the function of each part. The hand can only be grasped through the notion of the body; it is conceivable only within a consideration of the body. The body and all its limbs defines the hand; not only in structure and function is it related, but also in the form of being and action the body is present fully in the hand and can be determined through it and from within. Conversely, the hand is present in every part and function of the body, since the latter is related to the former in a necessary and living fashion. We could say that the living body is extensive, indeed, every part of it—as distant as it may be to all others; and at the same time, we could say that it is intensive, i.e., every part is present in the whole being. Moreover, every limb of the body is in itself unique and at the same time in the whole. Here, there seems to be a different idea of space than in the mechanistic, merely coordinated system. We experience this relationship in the form of our experience within a living, spatially ordered body. Its spatial being we experience as a peculiar being-within of coordination and cooperation. It is possible for an organic structure, which includes spatially separate elements to live, even when the carrier of its existence is inorganic.

Existence and coexistence are dependent on one another yet separate. They are separate not just in the sense that they are separated parts of a structure, microscopically arranged close together, as though the living seed already contains in potentiality a life form—to be later fully unfolded in a microscopic unity—but in a simple inexistent and living coexistence, which is the quality of a living substance. This living substance is in itself logically and biologically ordered.[8]

---

7. See the meditations of the *Gestalttheorie* ("Gestalt-Theory"). For example Max Wertheimer, "Über Gestalttheorie" [On Gestalt-Theory] and "Drei Abhandlungen zur Gestalttheorie" [Three works on Gestalt-Theory], *Symposion* 1, booklet 1, (Erlangen, 1925): 39ff.; A. Wenzl, "Der Gestalt und Ganzheitsbegriff in der modernen Psychologie, Biologie und Philosophie" [Concept of Gestalt and Wholeness in Modern Psychology, Biology, and Philosophy], 1931.

8. Translator's note: This is a difficult passage, even in German. I think "inexistence" (which is also a German neologism) means "to be in." He counter poses it with "coexistence" (being with), so he speaks about the difference of "being in" and "being with." In a way, Guardini tries to illustrate his statement here by pointing out a very special "way of being."

The same is true regarding chronological forms. A song, for example, contains a form. This form [Gestalt] realizes itself in the chronological succession of tones. Every part of the melody brings forth part of the form. When the third stanza of a song is sung, the first and second are not relegated as past; they remain present, *there*, concomitantly understood. Likewise, stanzas yet to come are already *present* and understood. The previous and the latter stanzas are not present in thought in the form of a memory or in anticipation; rather, the form is as a whole fully present in every part of the song, even if each part only completely realizes one or another part of it. The melodic form realizes itself in the succession of one part after another, but every part of the succession contains the entirety of the timely form. The form is realized separately and individually in each distinct part.

The same is true for the progression of life. Form appears and realizes its teleological unity within the course of a life; every part is related to the whole. The coherence of life derives from the original unity of an inner form of life, which is irreducible to its parts. Through this inner form, the individual stands within himself, realizes himself, and becomes one with himself over the course of his life. This organic succession, this process of the organic form, which becomes evident over the course of a life, relates differently to time than a sequence of merely mechanical events succeeding one after another. A whole is realized in the succession: the form of our lives. It contains the entire line of bodily development, psychological unfolding, the line of work, and within it—carrying and being carried—the line of fate, the foreordination of life. This is all ordered in succession, yet it remains wholly manifest in every individual instance: partial events resting in the whole. We experience this in the way in which a day or a year passes by, or the whole period of our life can become simultaneously present to our consciousness: through teleological and melodic form and unity.[9]

---

[9]. Fundamental problems arise here: What is the meaning of the given event as seen from this point of view? Is it something that is added and not immediate to the form [Gestalt]? What is historical which cannot be deduced from essence? Furthermore, how can we confront a free action with the teleological and functional whole? How do person and freedom relate? We are dealing with the problem of history as something integral, but also as something factual, something that is not necessary in its very essence. We are likewise dealing with history's relation to the person, not only his psychological and physiological dimension. Finally, we are dealing with the problem of providence in its widest sense.

An obstacle appears as soon as we exit the closed realm of the *individuum* and start to think about the whole.[10] Is the concept of the unity of life applicable to a multitude of lives? In so far as this multitude is a *sum*, no, it cannot. However, there is a sort of multitude that is not a sum. Families, nations, and finally, humanity are difficult to grasp as entities, but are nonetheless super-individual entities, having lives of their own with respect to the individuals of which they are composed. Each one's organic form realizes itself through its contemporary members and within a succession. Every type of community and society is a manifestation of this unity-structure and function and is present to the consciousness as an *organism*, even if only in a weak sense. The succession of passing events is *history*. In this sense—even if it is a weak sense—it is an organic event, not a merely mechanical one. (St. Augustine called history a *carmen pulcherrimum*, a "most beautiful song," which elapses over time with ordered parts.) Both, community and history, experience their highest intensification in the conception of the religious unity, the Church. She is in her contemporary source, as well as in her succession, an *organism*: *Corpus Christi mysticum*. As such she presents herself to the Christian consciousness.

The Church is also the fullness of all things human; contemporary to today, the spatially separate manifoldness of human experience; the succession of human events, which form an organic whole and can be formulated by the concept of organic space and organic time. According to its measure and intensity, as well as envelopment, every human life depends upon how much the wholeness becomes its structure and successive form of life. This is determined by one's conscious penetration of one's own standing-in-life, the consciousness of the essential power of the soul's personal life and the duration of one's memory; but also—beyond one's objective consciousness—by the strength and the way of self-experience, whereby every particular form is not seen as particular but as a general part of one's own being. The same is true for super-individual unities: family, nation, state, Church. Each one depends on the liveliness with which each individual stands in relation to the whole, in how far the individual can experience the whole as a reality of life. An individual's participation will always depend on the strength of his *memory* and his capacity to recollect

---

10. See the excursus on page 118.

the surrounding forms into his own. It will depend on the individual's width and sensitivity with which he is a *member* and *phase* of that whole.

The way of the individual toward the super-ego and the super-presence, the experience of timely and spatially removed events in the here-and-now of the present, could be understood as happening immediately. However, such would presuppose capacities that are not normal for humanity: parapsychological capacities, such as the skill of clairvoyance. I myself cannot judge if this particular capacity actually exists. Serious research suggests that it would be difficult to completely discard the possibility of things of this nature existing. Perhaps it is possible to be in one place and to see what happens in another, or to live at a certain hour and yet understand what happens in another. Neither would work by way of external mediation—that is, by way of a spatially timely distancing of the means of communication and message. They would instead occur immediately, through an immediate givenness in the here and now. (We are dealing with, I repeat, events that are related to the lives of people as a whole, not just any event in nature.)

Either way, the significance of such parapsychic events in modern day would be the clairvoyant capacity to immediately understand the spatially timely distant and would increase an attitude in extraordinary measure, which already is rooted in an ordinary form in our cultural attitude as a whole. Our current relation to the past, to everything historical, seems too different than the way people of past centuries considered the times behind them. In those days men knew how relate to that which preceded them through knowledge, by way of text and inheritance, ruins, monuments, etc. More precisely, people knew that their connection to the past did not have a living character, but was only a relation of knowledge. The relation rested on the absoluteness of temporal distance, on mere post-ordination: historicism. In addition, to this relation—the second being additional since the former always remains the proper one—is added a second relation in which the structure of experience may be carried forward by way of something immediate. Naturally, this relation cannot be objective and absolutely immediate—one always knows about the past through messages, sources, and monuments. However, the nature of the way by which people, being informed through these channels, tends to form a relationship between them and the past tends to belong to another psychological species. This species seems to bear the character of the simple recognition of something given. What has happened is taken as something *present*, as something given in general, as the living historical substance that persists today. Caesar, Augustus, Thomas Aquinas, Rembrandt, Goethe are not something of the past that we can only know by way of monuments, which can only act upon us through the chain of causes leading into our present in such a way that all that is related to them returns to a past moment. Instead these personalities simply *are*. They do not bear the character of the *past*, or at least they do not exclusively bear the character of the past. We know as much of them as sources tell us; we know also that they existed in the past. What I am explaining neither suggests the clairvoyant cancellation of the limit of time, nor does it argue for the chaotic amalgamation of the order of time. I am speaking about the way in which we relate to them in an orderly fashion as past, a way in which our coming to know them is communicated through knowledge of a non-*historical* character: it is *immediate* knowledge of something living and given. In addition, the clairvoyant recognition shows, as exception and borderline case, the intentional direction according to which the collected attitude of our time is moving.

We begin to experience all events regarding humanity, history, as a whole. The past is experienced as something super-historical and timeless, something living and passed on. Those persons and freedoms that are about to come—are not forgotten!—are announced in the present. The event of human history as a whole appears as a great teleological order, as a melodic form [Gestalt]. Within it, everything is carried onwards, everything is handed down. We detect the sense of history in the continuation of realized teleology, form, and melody (the divine world-plan, providence, and kingdom). Just as in a song previous tones are actually passed yet contained in the present moment by a continuing existence of the living melodic form and the way in which the present tone follows the previous and carries on into the next, so our historical experience relates to the present. That which we have heard about from the past is transformed like a tone adopted within a new melody—the current teleological phase is preconditioned by something previously realized.

This is all related to mankind and the super-individual unity of life, which carries the wholeness of political and cultural, as well as historical, context. It is the self-experience of the living organic humanity, which the individual realizes as the measure of width and power for his super-individual consciousness of life.

In this thought, there certainly lies a danger: the romantic-organizational conception of events, in which person and decisions are deprecated, historical uniqueness is veiled, and the tragic *past* of the historic deed is concealed. Of its own accord, the truth contains this danger, and you cannot encounter the danger by ignoring it.

It seems peculiar. All deeply un-historical attitudes remain confined within the time-atom[11] of the now and reduce everything that belongs to the past to mechanical functions separated by time and distance. In addition, these un-historical-attitudes, though possessing knowledge of and relations to the past, keep themselves outside of living continuity and living tradition. These very same attitudes long anxiously for the past—in an historical way—as it has been conserved, thinking it could only have been as real as the old texts and monuments suggest. Time that is considered historically cannot convey true historical presence or the creative present. Its affirmation of the present brutally slams everything past, which is of no scientific interest. Therefore, only the fragment of the present that is void of tradition is actually at work. Put another way, the present is only half-affirmed because the past within it is destroyed to make room for what is to come. We require a truly historical attitude that can establish a living connection to the past as it is handed on to the present. However, this historical attitude is always ready to sacrifice that which has been in the name of what is to come. Despite the monumental demise that surrounds us, we can affirm [the good], because we carry the historical past in our living being.

A similar proportionality exists in the spatial order. Just as the historical attitude relates the present to the chronologically distant, so the technological attitude can see what is spatially distant. This type of relationship is technological in character, and interprets movements toward tools, machines, and traffic from this perspective. There is a change here. Naturally, the distant remains distant, but we heard it through testimony, reached it by a movement, and acknowledge it by our instrumental

---

11. Translator's note: By "time-atom," Guardini means "moment" as a point in time. Thus referring to the moment as the part of something larger, the ongoing stream of history.

influence over it (apparatus). However, we can also stand in relation to the spatially distant in a different fashion. We sense that the space pertinent to man's existence is formed together in a unity. More precisely: we sense a unifying, spatially ordered form of the space related to man with its organic structure; at least we strive for an understanding of it, a struggle that is carried by the whole of humanity. This understanding of space supports geopolitical science. Areas of land and of the earth, rivers, seas, and mountains are understood as one—in relation to the people living in or near them—humanity, as a whole is understood in this unified space and through it. The human person experiences space, great and segmented, differing in quality and dynamics, within the complete human-historical form. Once more, this does not occur in a clairvoyant way. Clairvoyant knowledge about something distant is only an extraordinary case, which may be useful to form a more general relation to humanity as a whole. A different attitude must become evident in politics. It is the living consciousness of humanity extended in their living space, whose form is present in all areas—a sort of consciousness of mankind which is similar to historic memory of a people.[12]

Here I see an attempt for a new relation to the religious facts, which—positively laid out—we encounter in the liturgical mystery: a new capacity and willingness to see what has passed within present living actions and to see all that is spatially distant within present space.

No organic relation to space and time describes what happens in the mystery. In a certain way, our time comes close to the attitude, which begot liturgical forms and processes. Therefore, there is a temptation to understand them as the results of natural processes (for example, as results of the body-soul consciousness, the sense for symbol, etc.). However, to do so would confuse Christian liturgy with liturgical culture. This would touch the multiple attempts to build new religions: new myths, new cults, and so forth. All of this would derive from a deep misinterpretation. As *cultically* gifted as an era may be, no Christian liturgy can grow from it.

---

12. On this basis, a new historical-political consciousness must arise: on consciousness of the cosmic space and its relation to man; of human reality in its internal structure and mutual coexistence; the awareness of the living whole of history; of historical teleology and overall form in its relation to the now, and the now in its position to that. One must sense all of this and feel, too, how realities construct this whole; feel the whole, as a natural process and natural context, born out of necessities, at the same time as the given task of the free person; the individual as a whole and the whole as an individual—this is a prerequisite for living politics. (MGV note: These sentences were written in 1925!)

Christianity was not culturally hatched; it was positively revealed and posited in time. It corresponds to revelation, action, and positioning by God. It is history as seen by God. At its core, too, liturgy is not culturally constructed, but positively positioned by Christ, formed in the bosom of historical Christianity, recognized and placed by a legitimately ecclesiastical structure. Christian liturgy is super-natural, historically unique and positive, seen from God and from the Church. Either it is legitimate or it is nothing.

Through certain temporal conditions—including those developed above—access to the Christian mystery can be facilitated. According to its essence, it is not deducible from natural conditions but can only be posited and actively believed. It remains at all times a mystery—that is, the mystery of faith. However, perhaps specific times have a specific calling to unlock it, as others have a specific calling to unravel the dogmatic or juridical side of Christian reality.

In medieval thought, we find a concept that may gain new importance for us. Since it expresses an attitude, it is more than a concept: the *aeviternal*. This means the following: First, there is an *aeternum*, which is eternity. Thomas comments: *Aeternitas (est) mensura esse permanentis* ("Eternity is the measure of permanent being") (S. Th. I, q. 10, a. 5). Or we have the beautiful definition from Boethius, so dear to the Middle Ages: *Aeternitas interminabilis vitae tota simul et perfecta possessio* ("Eternity is the whole, simultaneous, and perfect possession of boundless life").[13] It is the eternal *now*: wholly fulfilled life. Second is the concept of the *aevum*, in its significance of *saeculum*, time. [The *saeculum*] refers to finite becoming and change, which "is measured by time . . . and has a prior and a later." Part of the event remains distinct from the other. It is not a *tota simul et perfecta possessio* [the simultaneously whole and perfect possession], not an exhaustive *now*, but the realization of a whole in successive parts. Third and finally, there is the concept of the *aeviternum*. This is the way in which the eternal and timeless coexists in time. God is eternal. His life stands in a fully exhausted, simple, and eternal now. He has no relation to time; time is created by him as the way of finite being. However, he coexists with all time. Time completes itself, carried by God, fulfilled by him, guided by him. The carrying, navigating act of God, his counsel and his providence,

---

13. Translator's note: *Consolatio philosophiae*, V, 6.

coexist with time, without being temporal themselves. This coexistence is the *aeviternum*: the concept contains that which is eternal, but which is related to time.

There is also the concept of *ubiquity*, which is omnipresence. God himself has no place. He creates space for form of finite being. Infinity is not the highest measure of space, but a prominence over all space-measures. As super-spatial, God carries, fulfills, and orders every spatial measure. The relationship of the super-spatial to the spatially measured is omnipresence.

There is an analogy from experience for both concepts. The soul is in itself not spatially delineated, and it is imperishable. It is the spiritual form of the spatial body, the teleology, melody, and flowing form of individual life. As such, it coexists, as a whole, in every part of the spatial body and in every length of time of an individual life. Its relationship to the spatially constructed body and the temporal passage of life are in finite correlatives to God's *aeviternity* and *ubiquity*.

That which is and that which happens are created, carried out, and fulfilled by God. He is eternal; his counsel and his work are manifestations of an eternal and simple act. In contrast, beings and events coexist aeviternally in history. Said otherwise, what happens historically and personally gains its final meaning by the fact that it fulfills God's image and will: it creates a *Kingdom of God*.[14] Even historically speaking, it gains its meaning by the super-historical. Once it reaches the eternal fullness of form and meaning, it itself is assumed into eternity, *into heaven*.[15] It becomes *aeviternal*.[16] Thus, it participates in the relationship of God to the world: it can become aeviternal and can coexist in history and with God. It is a mighty thought to think that human action—once it is oriented toward God—fulfills his will and that man can enter into his kingdom, gain super-historical meaning, super-temporal reality, and be able to participate in the relationship between God's thought of the world and his creative power and the actual world. The act of man can come into relation with all of history.

---

14. The words taken in their widest meaning.
15. The words taken in their widest meaning.
16. More precisely, no longer perishable; withdrawn from time.

If we can imagine this fact becoming reality in the consciousness of mankind—and I think that in some way this was so the Middle Ages[17]—then we will attain an attitude with immense power: humanity stands in time, but is oriented toward eternity. Human beings are conscious of the fact that they, while created as they are in history, perform actions that ascend into eternity. Their creative actions are redeemed of their temporality in eternity, in God's created relation to the world, in the will of his kingdom. Mankind has entered a history in which he can co-create. This is expressed in the idea of the *communio sanctorum*, the *community of saints* that our perspective makes easily understandable, and is also accessible through the practices of the supplication of the saints, indulgences, and many other things.

If we can look back at these thoughts from a distance and keep in mind that they are auxiliary to our primary concern, we will realize how they can aid us in understanding the liturgical mystery.

Time and space as forms of succession and the contemporariness of events and things are real. However, it seems that spatial and temporal separation—within a living human person—also exists as a principal unity. It seems possible for us to comprehend them as one within a living unity, though temporally and spatially separated. Obviously, this is only possible under conditions that carry for us the character of the extraordinary. Direct recognition of this would be clairvoyance.

As such, the extraordinary seems to be a borderline case which reveals within the total relation of the spatial-temporal toward this: the overcoming of history and technology, the mere mediation-relation toward the thing; the striving toward an immediate form of space and time which is—next to the mediated—understood in the living. Enough has been said in this cultural-historical attempt.

This whole study becomes more significant when put in a religious context: God, the undivided one, non-spatially eternal, coexists in all temporal and spatial events. Everything exists in him; he gives reality a base, creates it, and holds it in being. Thus, every spatial thing and temporal event leads in some way to God and from God. Whatever happens in God coexists in time: his counsel, his knowledge, his love, his grace. Whatever

---

17. A holistic understanding of time of the Middle Ages and its periodic eras aims at this. Also the permeating of life, legend, symbolism, etc.

happens with God as an end rises above the spatial-temporal in its order into *heaven*; this is possible because he wants it to be and he wants it to re-affect history in turn. Faith realizes this relationship. Revelation does not account for all that has passed, but all that is present. What happened in the past has indeed happened for all time; this applies to me too, to today, to the now. In its origin all time coexists with God, including, naturally, today. Faith focuses on the historical Christ, his person, his life, his words, his passion, and his resurrection. However, the focus on these events is not as though they were of the past, warranting only an historic relationship by way of testimony through a historical succession, but as events of the present. They were real in the past; they were not "ideas" or "myths"; they are truly parts of history. Since Christ was sent by the Father and, as the Son of God, fulfilled the will of the Father; and because he as the Godman resurrected in triumph and entered his glory sitting at the right hand of the Father whence he reigns as judge, therefore his redeemer-ship and redeemer life lives aeviternally, coexisting for all time. He is not in time, but he is the Lord of all time. After he has returned home, has entered eternity with his whole being, he returns back to history. Thus will begin his *parousia*, his return. He will return to every historical moment in which there was one who believed that "he is in Christ and Christ is in him."[18] He is with us "until the end of the age." Christ speaks to every man from the past, from Palestine, from the time of Augustus and Pilate; speaking to us simultaneously then and now. He is the redeemer of all and the Godman who has returned to eternity. He bound himself within time and space during his earthly historical life in order to "fulfill everything in justice" and place man before the mystery of God made man. Faith means not only believing in the immediate Christ, it also means that Christ immediately stands in me; to have faith is to believe that I am called by him.

---

18. Parousia, the belief in parousia: the conviction that Christ will come again, and will come *soon*, belongs to the essence of the Christian attitude more deeply than the merely historical interpretation of the New Testament tends to assume. The only question is *whence* the fact and belief of the parousia have shifted. The question of *where* in the overall existence of Christian life sits upon the expectation of the parousia, which at first seems to have been immediate-historical. It has become constitutive of and is related to the relationship in which the *aeviternal* Christ currently resides. In the relationship between faith and in its sacramental materialization, in mystery, not only is the historical past perceived and renewed as coexistent, but the future also begins. The essential content of the Christian future is the parousia. In a mysterious way, Christ has already come.

Our faith experiences currently a deep crisis. Faith relies on the soul's reaching into the past by way of historical mediation. Nevertheless, there is a danger that its contrary may come to the fore: from the historical, the soul could turn to an idealistic faith, which leaves history aside, proclaiming instead that one's freed experience, the idea and the sense of what happened, are the essential elements. Living faith may not relinquish any fragment of history. The fact that God entered history is decisive for Christianity. Nevertheless, faith does not rely on insights into historical source material. It does not approach history in a merely temporal manner as though we were to consider the objects of faith in a merely historic fashion. In point of fact, the object is *aeviternal* and omnipresent, related to the here and now. The Christian Church and the Christian soul live in the present kingdom of God. The Church is not oriented toward something merely past and bygone.

Enriching every relation in the faith both quantitatively and qualitatively, the liturgy teaches that whatever coexists *aeviternally* with all of history can enter history at any time, if it is the will of God. Christ's life and death are perfectly historical. Yet the acts of the Son of God who has passed into his glory are at the same time aeviternal. As such, his life can be grasped by faith. If it pleases God, then he can take his salvific action out of his coexistence and approach the faithful by entering anew into history: he can renew his salvific action. This salvific action is not to be taken in the sense of a historical duplication, a sort of historical doppelgänger, but in a proper, unique form that only faith can grasp; not just as a piece of the species history, but in its own reality: as *mystery*.

This being said, we have not engaged in subjective speculation; we have rather made an attempt to emphasize what of liturgical mystery we have discerned.

The category of the *aeviternal* can be grasped by philosophical meditation on the variable forms of the concept of being. Such belongs to the philosophy of history or of culture, in general. The aeviternal's proper meaning may only be understood through a religious relationship: the relationship that the person of faith has to the event of salvation. No deduction from natural presuppositions, whether psychological, historical, or philosophical, can arrive at the character of the relationship, which becomes deeper within the coexistence of the event of salvation and reenters history in the form of mystery.

Every attempt to deduce this will necessarily lead to magic.[19] The whole retains its proper sense only when it is the result of a positive placing of the divine. The category of mystery, as we have discussed it here, is neither philosophical nor historical, but theological. It is not a natural category, but one of divine revelation that is instituted by God, a category that is specifically Christian.

The institution of the Eucharistic is a divine establishment, as it was instituted at the Last Supper. The event culminates in the words "Do this in memory of me!" These words are not spoken to modern, abstract, senselessly thinking people, but to ancient, concrete thinkers, aware of the meaning of their bodies. They lived in an environment that was accustomed to the imagination of cultic mysteries; they were familiar with representations of religiously meaningful, albeit mythical, events in cultic forms. When these people remembered the event of the Last Supper, the moment and its atmosphere, the words of Christ, they could not but see in it an institution with the living seed of a mystery. They did not see it as a copy of an ancient mystery, or as something even comparable, but as something unique, that was bound to the figure and the essence of Christ, asserted by his sovereign, personal being. They used the general cultural traits to express themselves, as they used in general all that was useful to them. The momentum of the person of Christ, and the intensity and inner logic of his life, overwhelmed the people, especially after the events of Easter and Pentecost; whereupon the truth of his identity definitely resounded. The people had understood the mystery departing from the given, historical preconditions, since even they were included into the *fullness of time* and were necessary to build the novelty and the unique features of the Christian mystery into history and to form it accordingly. On the other hand, this uniqueness was so commanding and unmistakable that it could not be confused with anything else and it could not be synchronistically absorbed by preexisting cultic forms.

After Christ returned home, once his concrete presence no longer reigned dominant in the consciousness of the apostles, the inner living

---

19. Here we can see the radical difference between the realization of Christ and his suffering on the Cross and the mystery of magical evocation.

seeds of the Last Supper could unfold in a cultic fashion: in thoughts, mentality, attitude, and action. A trace of slow unfolding can be seen when we compare the story of the Last Supper with a passage from the Acts of the Apostles 2:42, 46: "They devoted themselves to the teaching of the apostles and to the communal life, to the breaking of the bread and to the prayers. [. . .] Every day they devoted themselves to meeting together in the temple area and to breaking bread in their homes. They ate their meals with exultation and sincerity of heart. . . . " The account is similar in Acts 20:7 when the celebration is tied to a specific day, Sunday. In 1 Corinthians 10:15 we see the celebration embedded in a true supper, the *Agape*. The author speaks of the dawn of abuses, which slowly creep in, separating the holy action from a meal of love and from it merely as a service to God. In this way, it will lose immediate interiority. However, anyone who is not governed by a certain religious romanticism—the romanticism of a community and the immediacy of its inner circle—sees that it had to come as a result. The living seed planted by Jesus in the words and actions of the Last Supper must have—as soon as it entered history—begun to unfold itself. A line follows from that moment through all of history, tied ultimately to the celebration of the Eucharist today.

The basic structure of the sacrifice remains: action done unto bread and wine and the recitation of particular words. What remains is for the sacrifice to be embedded into a larger event of prayer, as with the Passover celebration. What remains is a double orientation of meaning in the event. The direction of the sacrifice, as expressed in the words "given up for you," and the concomitant presentation of the Old Testament idea of "spilling the blood," tied to the blood of sacrifice, accordingly ties the New Testament to the new blood sacrifice. That is the meaning of the holy meal, eating and drinking as sacrifice and participation.

This action unfolds in an ever-richer way wherein specific forms and laws are initiated, as soon as such a seed of events enters the liturgical sphere. This is the proper logic of form, action, and the word. Let us attempt to propose some fundamental aspects of its essence.

Before we begin, we must affirm that the event in question is not repeated in a naturalistic way. Were it so, then it would be an attempt to create a historical doppelgänger, even if expressed merely in form. Rather, the concrete form of the action is transposed from the historical event into the cultic sphere. The mysterious form of appearance is not of realistic-historical nature that somehow points to an event past and recreates a past moment; instead it stands in itself, precisely as a properly cultic-liturgical event. Rather than present a naturalistic recreation, the form is stylized. Moreover, it is symbolic. There is no possibility of confusing it with an historic event. The faithful will never be compelled to see a copy of the Last Supper and the event of the crucifixion in the celebration of the Eucharist. The dimensions of the liturgical-mysterious and the historical-realistic-empirical are separated clearly by their forms of expression.

The essence of the formation of the liturgy is the idea that the *same* is not emulated, but that the *same* is progressively fit to the circumstances of a new environment—albeit resisting change by sticking to the intention of the original form. These moments happen simultaneously, to make them useful. However, at its core, the formation of mystery is in a certain sense a creative moment. (I am speaking about the psychological-historical side of the event. In itself, it is the instrument of the forming power of the Holy Spirit.) The complete essence of the Last Supper is contained in the indication "Do this in memory of me." It consists in the cultic-creative attitude and is emphasized according to the essence of liturgical formation. Everything is discarded which belongs to the historical-realistic form of appearance of the event as such. The essence of the liturgical event takes on the varying forms of the given liturgical-cultic sphere. The result is that—I repeat—we are not dealing with a *re-creation* of events, which would ever remain questionable, but with a transposition[20] of the essential core of the historical event into liturgical form.

The altar does not represent the table of the Last Supper; it is its sacred equivalent. The equivalent relation applies to the Church and Cenacle. The liturgical bread and the liturgical chalice do not re-create the bread and the cup of Passover, but they show unambiguously in their form that we are dealing with a transposition into the liturgical equivalent.

Even less so does the liturgist[21] re-create or imitate the person of Christ. The form, clothes, and attitude of the priest contain something

---

20. That the liturgical act does not fulfill the thirst for realistic representation has been the specific cause of the mystery play, which seeks a rich and concrete representation. However, here the artistic representation also consists of a transposition of one form into another, in this case into aesthetical form.

21. Translator's note: i.e., the person performing the liturgy.

strictly stylistic. They feel foreign and alien, things removed from their historical environment. Even the danger contained therein is easier to accept as the idea of imitation. If it were so, it would entail the sacrilege that a human being claims a special, personal relationship of identification with Christ. It would be an unbearable burden, which would demand tactfulness saturated with security to escape. Because we have to remain truthful and shy away from any danger in confusing the core of the mystery, we have to avoid veiling the identity of the present and historical event or reconstruct it as an historical or psychological celebration merely for personal edification. If, on the other hand, in faith it is given that the events are identical to mystery's reality, then the demand for perfect religious purity would require that the priest's action be strictly liturgical, even if this entailed that he be alienated from life and exercise a certain coldness. The carrier of sacred actions in the liturgy is not the priest's personality, nor a power bestowed upon him that is rooted in some special empowerment of the re-living and presentation, but the pure power of his office as organ of the Church. If we look closer, then we will see that all the elements of the liturgical act—attitude, clothing, and form—point to the switching off of all that is personal such that the liturgical actor may shine forth as the carrier of his office and the Church's power. Anything additional that derives from the personal engagement and power of representation in the *person* is—from this viewpoint—secondary.[22]

The same is true for the rest of the liturgy. The use of instruments, the forms [Gestalt] of the whole situation, the way the words are said and the actions done—none of these entail the recreation of the historical event, even less: the fuller the liturgy is and the more the faithful enter into the intention of the liturgy, the more it is true liturgy. This will be particularly important at the moment of consecration, the heart of the mystery, when according to the sense and demand of what happens, the event of the Cenacle becomes actually real. Here the whole contracts in the most stringent form. What is missing is any literal representation of the Passion.

By what has been said, more has been revealed: the unfolding realization of the historical past can externally enter history anew through mystery. Not just internally, spiritually—in that the living Redeemer will

---

22. Surely, the reader has heard a lot about the pride of priests. May the reader seek to understand what the above mentioned means in terms of sacrifice for the celebrant.

become present in this person and in this community—but also as external, historical action.

Since the given situation is historical, this liturgical agent will fulfill the sacred action in this city, in this church, on this specific day, and in this specific year. Likewise, it will be realized for these people, each in their own particular life and context. Thus every liturgical celebration represents a part of history, which is woven into the context of a before and an after, and is supported by living events and circumstances. The question remains: How can every event—itself a unique piece of history, which occurs and only fits within a very particular historical moment—be inserted into another historical *place*? Every attempt to devise a realistic re-creation would be anachronistic, an alien body and a repulsive disruption of the historical train of events. The liturgy is not supposed to represent something as for example a passion play. The latter only happens in the sphere of imagination. The onlooker steps out of his own temporal reality and into the past. No disruption of the historical continuity ensues—especially since the event of the play itself, as carried by real people, stands in the historic present. There is reality, a mystical one, but reality. How could such reality be inserted seamlessly into the present, historical context if it has the character of a representation?

Put otherwise: When every reality appears in the form of mystery, then it is liturgical action. Of its nature, it is non-realistic and stylized, thereby making it possible for it to be inserted into every historical situation, church, and state of mind in the total manifold places, times, and occasions. This is not to say that the form of the liturgical action is super-temporal. It can and may change, and depending on the times, be felt as something more or less alien. Still, this does not mean that the line of reality is broken in itself; we are dealing with different gradations of immediate experience. We are dealing with something fundamental: an effigy would be felt as something inherently impossible. The resurrection of past events is only possible when what happens occurs in an essentially unrealistic, symbolic form.

In this form, every event can insert itself into history, time and time again. When I, as the person I am, participate in the life that I participate in, in the celebration of a liturgical mystery, then this mystery enters into my life as part of my history. The same is true for the community that celebrates the mystery in its modern constituency.

If we truly penetrate this in thought, we will realize the significance that lies within. Mystery becomes history over and over again. It can trigger and express history, such as in the celebration of thanksgiving of supplication. It can form history, as it forms human beings who take part in history. It can turn history and be created in the hearts of those men who participate wholly within the contemporary moment.

Now we can say at last: the historical event of salvation appears in the form of mystery in history, time and time again. This means that there is continuous salvation. The mystery stems from the coexisting aeviternal work of God. Its sense of direction is to grip history ever anew and draw it into eternity; to take it out of its singularity and bring it into the reality of salvation. Because individual human beings and individual communities take the mystery into their lives, their lives are brought into the mystery and therefore into communion with God.

Excursus (see footnote 10, p. 102):

How does this relate to the person? In the core of this thought lies the danger that the person be reduced to a mere cell in a larger construct. The danger lasts only as long as one does not understand the qualitative relation of person to the whole. A person is not just an individualized fact, not a purely *privatum* something. The phenomenon of the person is composed of one's individual singularity as well as his relation to the community. The faithful person understands this, since he understands "person"—of which man is merely an image—as an image of the Trinity, the divine Persons which are by nature individual and communal. The personality of God is revealed to us in such a way that his personhood consists in the way he is in relation to himself. The first person is a person by being "father," i.e., a community member; the second by "son"; the third is "spirit," community affirming love. The community function is not merely attached to the individual-personal; rather, personal independence is truly founded in its unmistakable peculiarity by the way one stands in community. Community, in turn, is justified by the fact that it is formed by these unmistakably peculiar persons. For us, human persons, this is the cognitive starting point for reaching an understanding of the divine. In terms of being, however, the divine person comes first, the human remains his image. For the believer, then, the self-revelation of the divine form of person becomes a religious base for an insight into the nature of the person in general. It follows that the "isolated individual" does not exist. Perhaps he exists as a borderline case which serves to secure the fact of the individual in peculiarity. Nor does there exist a situation of absolute commonality in which the individual would be only an indistinguishable cell. This would also be a borderline case. What truly exists is the community-related individual and the person-related community. Yet there does remain the question: how is an "order of people" possible? The person is essentially unique. Can one combine one uniqueness with another and a third to form orders? This question starts with mere counting: that I say "two people" already startles me. Either I cancel out the personal and treat "men" in one shared category—as, for example, "birds"; then I am not counting true human beings, but something else altogether. Or I do address the personal—that is, man's unique essence—and then I must ask myself how I am "counting." Here lies the root of the problem. Either the ordering act of counting cannot happen, or what is counted is actually not that which I wanted to count in the first place.

This problem then continues through all the different relationships in which people can be connected to order—natural relationships: generation, birth, nutrition, education . . . ; purpose relationships: socialization of work, struggle, play . . . ; *Gestalt*-relationships: family, community, state . . . ; cultural relations: communication, instruction, education, spiritual giving and receiving . . . ; the same question everywhere. To put it superficially, let us summarize all human forms of similarity together in the concept of "society" and all forms of order in succession in the concept of "history." Then the question is: can people, personal acts, and personally created individuality come together in a true society and historical order? If we are aware that this order should not only contain human vitality by the fact that man is a living being and as is indicated in the Aristotelian term *animal sociale*, but also and especially because it is composed of persons? The problem seems often neglected; otherwise one would not be so free to speak of social and historical order with such liberty. As soon as we approach the problem from the viewpoint of order, then person and order seem to cancel each other out: In a way, "person" is canceled when there is true order, meaning that there is no person whatsoever. Alternatively, "order" is cancelled out if we take the individuality of the person seriously.

Now it is evident that there is personal order. So the concepts of order and the attitude that implements order, with which we are familiar, cannot be the only ones. In addition to the factual order, we have to adopt a concept of a special personal order. What this specific order of people consists of and in what the act realizing this order consists do not seem to be clear to the theoretically or practically minded.

Perhaps this problem is the deepest cause of the social and historical crisis of our time. Over the past three centuries, the person has become aware of his proper individuality. This feeling is probably very overwrought, precisely because it is something that is still at risk. The person feels that he is being treated as a non-person. This is not because order is demanded of him, but because the form of order into which he is brought and the form of the order-realizing act which is directed at him, comes from what is factual and therefore it is something which contradicts the person's essence in its quality. (For example: In the state, the generally prevailing order is based on the idea of an establishment that holds the masses together, forms them, and organizes them into a desired form. In history the individual is cancelled out when looked at through the eyes of evolution; evolution only fits impersonal beings because it treats species in which individuals are only generic carriers. Both ideas are taken from the impersonal perspective and seem to be easily transferrable to people. However, both actually ignore the person or try to extinguish him by treating him as a non-person.) Today's man feels deep distrust toward, even resistance to, the demands of the state, family, school, business, technology, etc. This resistance is basically directed—there is even an anarchical component in this mindset—not against the order itself; not against authority and obedience itself; yes, not even against the sharp and decisive strain of this demand, since our time especially demands authority. It would be a misunderstanding, also, to think that real authoritative order, the real lawful law, is discarded because its place is taken by an order of performance, rank, or personal trust (for example, the "leader" instead of the "official"). Man's resistance addresses the quality of the order; it wants to go against its thingly character. It goes against the fact that authority and tradition ignore the quality, measure, spirit, and attitude of the person and treats him as a thing. See footnote 29 in chapter 2. So it is a matter of seeing the order that is at the special service of the people. What must be assured is the realization of the order that does specific justice to the person. Should this happen, the idea of order may, theoretically, lead to its utmost consequence and have the most pointed effects. It is all a question of proper measure. What is decisive for the qualitative is that there be an order of persons.

The all-seemingly irresolvable problems can be untangled through the concept of thingly order. Initially, of course, these problems will only be brought out in terms of their dynamics: the problem of the state as an order of people; the problem of history as an order of relationships between successive personal forms, deeds, and fates; the problem of authority and independence, of education and self-growth, of guilt and punishment, etc. (Perhaps the specific category of law will also become clear here: the value of the right objective order among persons.) All of these questions have been forcibly simplified under the rule of the conceptual order of the subject, and thus led to apparent solutions. Hence there continues to be inadequacy in these theoretical and practical solutions and the person deeply distrusts them; hence the mutually corresponding extremisms of authority and autonomy, dictatorship and rebellion. These are signs that solutions have been sought at the wrong level.

Thus, should we want to address the contemporary problems in a proper manner, a solution cannot be sought based on the way that has been done before. We must look for a solution on a more profound level. {MGV note: See Romano Guardini, *Letters from Lake Como*, letter 9 (Grand Rapids, MI: Eerdmans, 1994), and the study "Über Sozialwissenschaft und Ordnung unter Personen" [About social studies and the order between persons], in *Unterscheidung des Christlichen* (Mainz, 1963), 34ff.; also "Welt und Person" [World and person] (Würzburg, 1955; Mainz/Paderborn, 1988).}

CHAPTER FOUR

Historical Action and Cultic Event

I

The upcoming *Eucharistic Congress*[1] brings up certain questions, especially for those who are far from understanding the intentions of the congress. One of these questions is addressed in this chapter, based on my presentation. The efforts of the congress pertain to the core religious event of the Church, the celebration of the Eucharist, which is colloquially called *Holy Mass*. The questions are: (1) What is the foundation of this celebration in Sacred Scripture? (2) On which event therein is it based?

All four Gospels speak about the leading representatives of the Jewish people's refusal of Jesus' message; moreover, they speak about wanting to get rid of him altogether. The spirit of his mission forbids him to protect himself with force or with deviousness, likewise to flee into safety. He must stay and accept what is to come—that is, his death.

Now, the last time Jesus dwelt with the close circle of his disciples was in a room put at his disposal for the Passover commemoration meal. The community of the master and his disciples was something very intimate, even more intimate than the family. The gathered members were all filled with somber solemnity.

According to Jesus' intention, this evening was not merely a farewell. In the Gospel of St. Luke, it is written: "He said to them, 'I have eagerly

---

1. MVG note: This talk was given in 1960 at the 37th Eucharistic Congress in Munich in the Bayerischen Rundfunk.

desired to eat this Passover with you before I suffer'" (Lk 22:15). What was it that gave that last gathering such weight beyond personal sentimentality?

One spirited text, which time and time again shows how much man is worth, speaks about the last unification of a master with his disciples: Plato's *Phaedo*. In it, Socrates is the master. He is condemned and, on the same evening, he is handed over to die. Athenian law allowed him, nevertheless, to be surrounded by his pupils in order to give them his last message, the epitome of the teaching he has given them over the course of years.

This height of his wisdom can be summarized in this way: what is essential for man is his soul, and the soul lives from the truth. Truth can be recognized when the will is put to it in all sobriety. Therefore, seek, and you will find it. What gives meaning to man's life is the Good. This Good can be realized. Therefore, strive to attain it more than anything else. In all other things, do not follow me. Socrates himself is not significant, only the Truth and the Good. This lesson cannot be taught by the ways in which scientific truths can be taught. Were that the case, it would just be known, but not truly appropriated. Only you yourself can find and win it; it is everyone's personal responsibility. Socrates can only vouch for it by his life and his death: he gives sense to being—while he as a person remains alien to your sense of life.

Jesus thought differently. In St. John's Gospel, he says: "Without me you can do nothing . . . " (Jn 15:5). And again with Matthew: "No one knows the Father except the Son and anyone to whom the Son wishes to reveal him" (Mt 11:27). Further, what is written here, transforms from a mere recognition into a call to action: "No one comes to the Father except through me . . . " (Jn 14:6). And another time: "I am the way, the truth, and the life" (ibid.).

Mighty words, but not yet the most audacious. As in Capernaum, when he speaks of the Bread of Life—that is, of that which makes existence possible and meaningful—dissent against his preaching sinks deep into the circle of his disciples. He says: "I am the living bread that came down from heaven; whoever eats this bread will live forever." And further: "and the bread that I will give is my flesh for the life of the world." Though part of the audience protests, he does not mitigate what he has said, but emphasizes: "Whoever eats my flesh and drinks my blood has eternal life, and I will raise him on the last day" (Jn 6:51, 53, 54).

Outrageous words, especially keeping in mind the inflated strictness with which the people of the Old Testament rejected any attempt to see divine sense in any human form. We can understand how part of his audience, not trusting him in full faith, would separate themselves from him for good: "This saying is hard; who can accept it?" (Jn 6:60).

What does all of this mean? It means that there is no Christianity without Christ. Not just because revelation can only exist if there is someone to reveal it, but also because he is inexorably tied to his revelation. There is no Christian truth that can be separated from him; no Christian wisdom of life that can persist separated from him, because then we would be separated from the essence of being. Christianity is Jesus Christ and communion with him. In him, God has come to us; through his actions and death the guilt of the world is expiated and the meaning of being is transformed. In him, the way leads back to God.

II

What Jesus did on the evening before his death is the final consequence of his teaching and the truth about salvation. He does not just summarize his teachings, nor does he entrust his apostles with the duty of fulfilling all that remained unfulfilled; instead he collects everything into one through the mysterious action by which he gives himself to his friends—*giving* in a way that is signified by the natural symbols of food and drink.

In his First Letter to the Corinthians, St. Paul summarizes his eyewitness testimony in this way: "For I received from the Lord what I also handed on to you, that the Lord Jesus, on the night he was handed over, took bread, and, after he had given thanks, broke it and said, 'This is my body that is for you. Do this in remembrance of me.' In the same way also the cup, after supper, saying, 'This cup is the new covenant in my blood. Do this, as often as you drink it, in remembrance of me'" (11:23–25).

This text—as well as the texts of the four Gospels—highlights what is essential: as the ultimate and final fulfillment of what he came to preach and to do, Jesus gave to his Apostles his own life as the reality and power of new life.

This is in no way merely *imaginary*—such as in the way symbol can be a sort of participation according to a certain mindset—but it is meant in the ancient way of concretization, as embodied reality. To understand this, one has to understand the phenomenon of the cultic sacrifice, which is present in all ancient religions, and which in the Old Testament is purified and related to a personal God. The world is God's property; whatever man has, he receives from God's hand. The most intensive form of possession is food; the meal as an act is basically the consummation of food and drink received from an altar—that is, from a sacrifice. Now Jesus says: this sacrifice, that is me. He goes to die, not as a merely personal fate that he could escape, but as a mission in the name of all. His death expiated the guilt of humanity and initiated a new beginning of being. Through his sacrifice, he gives himself to those within whom he shares bread and wine as the nourishment of new life.

This is not intended to remain a unique event, closed within what happened that evening, but is supposed to extend through time.

As he did, so his own should do. Thus, he must come into *memory*, and his command is to be obeyed through the repetition of his action. Memory becomes—as shown in the Acts of the Apostles and the First Letter to the Corinthians—the center point of life for those who belong to him—the community that is called *Church*.

The word *memory* has a peculiar sense here. It entails more than the mere recollection of something in the past through thoughts, revelation, worship, or some other way. Indeed, that which was done by Jesus in the past is supposed to become truly real. The holy meal ought to continue throughout time so that in it the very same reality created by Christ's words in the communion he shared with his disciples may resurrect. The shudder of awe which permeates the First Letter to the Corinthians (11:17 ff.), the diligence of the holy order—which has become clear in the *Didache* (a writing of the first century)—shows that the Church is not predominantly based on a teaching but on a reality—that is, on the ever renewing presence of Christ in her midst.

III

For a moment, let us set aside the problems of faith, which result from this teaching, as we cannot address them here. We are interested in another question: How can this commandment be followed appropriately?

Appropriately, first in a general sense, means to protect the believer from any sense of impropriety or embarrassment in treating something holy. In a more specific sense as well, since what we are dealing with is also a unique historical action, the question is: in which form can this become a community's continuous core event, which endures through numerous centuries and various cultures without its central concept being reduced to a mere *idea*?

Let us do what is always good to do when we want to inquire into something in great detail. Let's restrict the scope of our inquiry and thoroughly exclude anything that could cause confusion.

What we cannot mean by this is that the historical event is repeated. History is a succession of unique moments of which each one is ultimately in the past immediately upon its enactment and can only continue in its effects. The consummation of Jesus' mission could never mean that what has passed can happen for a second or third time—in any case, this would be sacrilegious.

On the other hand, we also cannot mean that the faithful gather around, remember what has happened, and receive spiritual edification from this memory—in the way the Passover meal in the home community recalls the event from which the Old Testament originated—that is, freedom from Egyptian captivity. That would be a merely psychological-spiritual representation; never has the living Church doubted that what happens in the Eucharistic celebration is something entirely different from a re-thinking and re-living of the events. On the contrary, it is understood as reality. Through the celebration, that sacrifice, which happened once and for all, becomes present.

We also do not mean that a past event is mimicked. This has been done time and time again, for example, in passion plays, which, using dramatic means, try to bring the events of the past before the eyes of the present. Ignoring the uncertainty that is always connected to such attempts, we still have to admit that even in the case of a seriously pious approach, the content of the event is always theater; it is dramatic art. However, we are dealing with reality.

What opens before us in Jesus' intention and the action of his Church is, therefore, something unique, which cannot be contained in psychological or aesthetical content. For what happened to be represented ever anew throughout time, presenting the essential core of the Church's life in history and people's lives, must be founded on the founder himself. It is liturgy.

Every form of cult, which has developed out of Jesus' institution, can thus be understood. In his divine omnipotence, he has willed and made it so that something past can be present through time in each given moment, always in a new way: a real way, for which we rely on his word alone. All of this happens in the celebration of the Eucharist, which translates literally to *thanksgiving* or the *thankful commemoration*. When the celebrant, the head of the community—first the apostles, then the bishops, then the priests ordained by the bishops—speaks the words which Jesus once spoke over bread and wine in the assembly of faithful, then for the Church faithful, Christ and his death are present in the contemporary hour coming from of eternity. By the action, which he once fulfilled and which is resurrected in that moment, he offers himself up of his own accord for the salvation of the living community. Not just his truth, not just counsel, for example, and loving attention, but himself.

Perhaps you ask yourself—especially those of you belonging to non-Christian circles—is not all of this just a pious fairy tale? Religious fantasy that has no relation to reason and reality? Allow me to bring to your attention an example, which may be helpful to better understand what I mean.

It is part of the fundamental reality of human beings that an individual comes forth from the lives of parents, that the mother carries, bears, nourishes, and watches over the child during the early years of development. Each of us has a personal being, which—a paradox of our existence—grows to be strong and proper out of the purity and enrichment of our mother's self-giving.

This relation of self-giving takes some time to establish and is then transformed in a spiritual way, which is difficult to explain. Should someone say that there should be a symbol that expresses life-long self-giving, would this thought be so nonsensical? Would it not correspond to a true desire about which poets and wise men have spoken profound words?

Repetition of this past would obviously not be possible because the past is past, and one cannot return to the mother's womb nor the days of childhood. Nevertheless, what would happen if God himself wanted to enter into such living relationship? The idea of *rebirth* belongs to the essence of every religion: the transformation of an old and used-up life into a new one by some numinous power. When God tells us that he wants to give himself to humanity so that we may have life from his life, life in the most pure form, what would happen? True, this promise would not be understandable, but would it not touch upon something in us which is deeper than reason? We are speaking about such a promise. It has been given; therefore, it is revelation. Our acceptance of this promise and our courage to live with it is called faith. This is the backdrop of what we call the *celebration of the Eucharist*.

IV

The unique historical event of the evening before Christ's death has entered into an ever-renewed cultic event. A change had to happen for this to be possible, not only in the sacred reality itself, but also in the form of the event. The change is so profound that the onlooker may not even recognize the original event at first glance. It is a complex problem to which a whole science—liturgiology—is dedicated. Let me indicate the path upon which, over the course of centuries, what we call today the celebration of the Eucharist has been formed.

A meal was hosted by a religious leader together with his disciples. The mission of "Do this in memory of me" was originally an event, referring to the sharing of the meal that held the links of the small community together: the *Agape* or the meal of love (cf. Acts 2:42; 1 Cor 11:20). In the measure in which the community grew—as can be imagined—a multitude of difficulties arose: social tensions, personal problems, abuses, and the like. The First Letter to the Corinthians speaks of this. The commemorative event separated from this meal took on a life of its own.

A transformation was introduced which, through its form, asserted a necessity which, in turn, warranted changes in style.

The original place was a room in one of the large private houses of the time and which may have served for meals on other occasions. In early forms of the liturgy, this turned into a room that was separated from ordinary use and served a purely religious function. An ancient source, i.e., the Acts of the Martyrs, records that a person of high social standing offered a house for this purpose and that the bishop *consecrated* it for this specific use.

Reluctance to use such a house which was characterized by its private quality, while being useful in times of persecution, surfaced repeatedly in the first centuries. When this practice ceased, proper cultic buildings emerged: churches. This change obviously influenced the form of the commemorative celebration as well: it definitely lost its private form and gained the stylized and severe form of an official gathering. The interior atmosphere of the event also changed. The Last Supper gathering in Jerusalem was characterized by a profound movement. Jesus knew that his earthly fate had come to a culmination and this induced a seriousness that took hold of his apostles and is expressed in St. John's Gospel most markedly. Among the apostles, the feeling of looming danger was paired with wondering what the master would do when his mission was completed. Jesus himself acted with full knowledge and he took initiative that proved to be essential; the apostles would only understand this later. Therefore, an all-encompassing incomprehension loomed over them, a deep perplexity.

The mood changed after Jesus' passing. The sense of seriousness and interior participation remained the same. The immediate experience of a past event was replaced by religious mystery. The "Now we are together with the master . . . he knows what will happen . . . we do not know . . . egregious events will transpire . . . he speaks of betrayal, and all can be lost . . . " is replaced with the awareness that their mission is to realize the commemoration, meaning participation by faith in something that historically has passed, but that is present in a cultic form in the here and now. The *past* of the event stands before the eternity of God; out of eternity, it enters this hour. This is the—more or less conscious—foundational tenor of the celebration whereupon time is embedded in eternity and the here and now rises into transcendence.

Correspondingly, the appearance of the act changed. Originally, the master was present in his earthly form, directly and just as he had lived with his followers. Then he pronounced his mission, "Do this in memory of me," and a representative now acts for the consummation of this commandment. First, it was the apostles in the early community, then the bishop, and once Christianity and the Church had spread, it became the priest, ordained by a bishop, and in one word: the celebrant.[2] The quality of his action is expressed in a peculiar way: by speech. The literal words can be read in the Canon of the Mass. What Jesus did is written there: "On the night he was betrayed, he took the bread in his holy and venerable hands." As Jesus did, so the celebrant imitates. Then he speaks the words that Jesus spoke from the first person perspective: "Take this all of you and eat from it: this is my body." The priest says "my," but the one who truly and really acts and speaks is the eternal Christ. It would be a sacrilege to think that a man speaking and acting out of his own accord could do that which surpasses all human power. It is Christ who speaks and acts. Christ is not visible standing there, nor is he *impersonated*; he stands invisibly behind the acting celebrant and fulfills the mission. The religious act of the community consists in beholding in faith what is transpiring, a meal. The table, as well as the food and drink, have changed their appearance over the course of history: The house table turns into an altar. The bread that is taken from the table and broken into pieces is reduced to the smallest fitting form, the Host. The cup, once filled with wine and passed from hand to hand, receives now only a small amount that is solemnly poured into an ornate chalice.

Realistic forms transform into stylized ones, which should not draw attention to themselves, but which ought to open the inner glance of the community to what faith believes to be there. The consummation is a sort of *spiritualization*, yet it retains the material element, if even in the smallest measure, in order to avoid evaporating into the ideal. It is linked to concrete things: bread and wine. The sense of incarnation, of God's entering into the earthly-human sphere, persists, but in a denser cultic form that demands awe.

Liturgical dress has also changed. At first it was solemn, but still from things of common use. Slowly it grew more sacred—as is quite evident in style, since the style has remained unchanged in its ancient form. The dress is cut in a way that is incompatible with daily life. To the extent that it is

---

2. The German here is "Liturge," which would be rendered as "Liturgist." But RG does not mean the "scientist that deals with liturgy" but the celebrant. Therefore the correct translation of "Liturge" should be the "celebrant."

possible, it is sewn of precious fabric and ornament, and absolutely must not be used for profane purposes. Every piece of liturgical dress carries a symbolic, cultic sense that we must understand intellectually in our experience, though the faithful of the past could recognize them more immediately. From this we can also deduce how we ought to handle liturgical vestments when, for example, the bishop is dressed in them before a solemn liturgy.

What it means to maintain proper posture and perform certain gestures is transformed as well. At the Last Supper, these followed according to the nature of a meal, the meal of a religious master with his disciples. Jesus performed the gestures of an Old Testament father of the house presiding over a festive meal—obviously made unique by the persona who has entered the moment from all eternity. The disciples, mere human beings, were deeply moved and perplexed, trying in vain to understand what would happen. As the liturgy developed and become more stylized, it lost its original realistic character.

The rubrics concerning postures and gestures became ever stricter, steadily tipping the balance toward stylization and away from the movements of everyday life. Their meaning came to rely on symbolic forms, rather than on the realization of practical actions for practical purposes. This difference is crucial. It is the foundation of possibility for onlookers to join their own postures and gestures of symbolic meaning in the right relationship whereby the onlookers may understand their meaning and—seizing on the moment—reach the religious experience of what they express. Everything seems somewhat unnatural, theatrical, and senseless to a participant [in the mystery] who does not reach this point.

For the faithful too, postures and gestures have specific forms: solemn standing, kneeling, bowing, the sign of the cross—all of these gestures and actions involve the person who enacts them in the liturgical event.

Liturgical language is a phenomenon that warrants special attention. Originally, it was spoken in the common tongue. Over time, it also transformed into something distinct from everyday life.

Greek was the first tongue used in the liturgy, and it remains in remnants even today, for example, in the *Kyrie Eleison*. In the measure in which Rome's Church has proven dominion, the Latin language took over. That this language is no longer commonly spoken gives special emphasis to the liturgical event, and marks its difference from daily use. For the longest time, that liturgical language was in itself a moment in which mystery appears. Recently, through the efforts of the Liturgical Movement to bring the event more into the immediate life of the community, consciousness of the importance of the vernacular has been emphasized and the vernacular has come to be used ever more readily. It is interesting how today, especially in America, this importance is recognized and accentuated.

These reflections should point out how the event of which the Gospels speak has turned into that what we call today the celebration of the Eucharist. It is the way of transformation, which the external form of the Last Supper had to undergo a transformation—a tranformation from the singular unique historical event into an ever-renewing spiritual core event, which became the heart of the Christian Church's life.[3]

---

3. MVG note: Further reflections on this subject are discussed in chapter 3 of this book, "The Liturgical Mystery."

CHAPTER FIVE

A Word Regarding the Liturgical Question

PREFACE

After Guardini's "A Word Regarding the Liturgical Question" was published for the first time as a manuscript, it seemed desirable that it should be made accessible to all those whose spirits have been seized by the liturgical cause. The author has reformulated his thoughts and made fine adjustments. I commend this mature writing and let there be no debate, I convey it with my warmest wishes. I could not imagine a more felicitous introduction for the resolution of liturgical questions by true specialists under the guidance of the bishop.

Mainz, Feast of All Saints, 1940
Albert Stohr, Bishop of Mainz

****

Esteemed and most reverend friend,

You have been asking for an account of the basic principles, which are most important for the judgment of some liturgical questions for some time now.[1] Such an account is not easy since the elements are entangled and much is still in flux. Regardless, I want to attempt it—particularly since

---

1. MVG note: For the given reason, Romano Guardini wrote this letter to his friend the Most Reverend Bishop Albert Stohr of Mainz. He had an eminent effect in the liturgical *political* situation at the time. The MVG editors believe that for the sake of documentation, but no less its current meaning, it should be reprinted here.

with it I can give a sort of a testimony myself of the thirty-five years that have passed since I began with my theoretical and practical work.

What we meant with the very imprecise expression *liturgical movement* was not a united movement. The core of responsible people within it set out to bring the sacred service to the state of purity and purpose, which it must have in order to give God glory and introduce the faithful into the richness of the world of grace. Some one-sided and peculiar things were tacked on to this main intention, which darkened the true sense of it all. About twenty-five years ago [1915] a liturgical "amateur" might have thought that the movement was some historically minded people's attempt to dig out all liturgical texts and antiquated forms ill-fit to modern reality. Or that the intention of some aesthetically-minded cliques was to form religious life according to their wishes and to create a world of liturgy alternative to the parish community, and that this desire rested at the core of the movement.

Such opinions cannot in good conscience be retained today. Everyone unbiased knows that the liturgy is neither an historical nor an aesthetic antiquarianism, but something plainly essential—that is, the official liturgy of the Church, grown from the core of Christian history, and the *law of prayer*—as the old formula calls it—in an indissoluble connection with the *law of faith*. Frictions can be found everywhere, even in the liturgical movement, the true end of which was important and necessary. In gradation of importance, the intention that the faithful be introduced into the liturgical life of the Church barely falls short of the necessity of introducing them to the truth of Christian faith. Indeed if one takes a closer look, it will be evident that the essential recognition of this truth can only unfold in the world of liturgical life.

Over the course of the last years, every impartial person could have witnessed that the age of caretaker of souls came to an end. Special methods, which had previously been appropriate, had lost their effects. On the one hand, because circumstances changed; on the other, and primarily, because in general the way people thought and felt transformed. The time of those approaches had passed, and it would be fateful to ignore this event and see these temporary and changing methods as part of the essence of the Church. If my assumptions do not deceive me, then in the future the care of souls will not be limited to the essentially religious.[2] Thus, it is of

---

2. MVG note: This letter was written during the time of the Nazi terror.

the utmost importance to form the essentially religious dimension of mankind with absolute purity and strength. It should not be left to dwindle into the merely *practical*. It should not be allowed to slide into the merely edifying and the excessively moral. The whole richness of revelation's truth must fulfill it. The biblical word and theological thought must be its guiding principles. The Christian image of perfection must truly be a great ideal, which, at its core, invokes great enthusiasm. The sacred, sense-filled symbol of the Church must illuminate it. Her sense for community must support it.

For this to happen, first and foremost, definitively and necessarily, the liturgy must be able to unfold in the way in which and to the extent that it demands. We have already pointed out its limits, but we must now clarify an essential point first: The center point of ecclesiastical life will always remain the altar—at least it should be. Perhaps, it will not merely be the central core of the liturgy, but indeed will signify the epitome of liturgical life. Much depends on that which happens on the altar and what emanates from it into the life of the family and the individual. Therefore, the altar must be understood in its richest sense and highest form. Naturally, all of this must be directed toward the living care for souls. Care for the liturgy must be linked to the parish community, as it is in its reality. It must aim at the needs and see its possibilities and cannot demand from it anything that is against its essence. The community, in turn, should be entrusted with expressing what lies within it, with all its willingness and its capacities—and that are much more than many a *practical thinker* will admit.

However, how can we speak of a *liturgical question*? If liturgy is what we have just said it is, then it should be the self-evident basis and form of religious life! That is central. Yet the liturgy is a historical reality and as such has all the features of something that grows and changes, of something that generates *questions*. Questions arise such as: Are the forms and texts of the liturgy that originated at one specific time valid for the future? Will some psychological and symbolic motives come to be emphasized in the wrong way if essential forms change? And other questions of this sort should be considered. In the early days, the liturgy determined the whole life of divine worship. Gradually, manifold religious sentiments, first of groups of people and later of individuals, surfaced and created new and special forms. Compared to those, the liturgy as the official cult of the Church seemed to stand in stark contrast, and, naturally, questions arose:

How did these religious dimensions relate to one another?[3] Where do we find the essential elements? Which are the limits? The list of concerns went on. All these questions are deep reaching and much entangled. To probe them means attempting to discover a theory of the history of Christian religious life. I have only pointed them out to make apparent the background against these things of which we are speaking unfolded. Here I must again limit myself. I want to stress two, one-sided polarizations that appeared at the beginning of the liturgical movement and the dangers lying within them. *Catchphrases* cannot be avoided here. Since they easily disfigure the cause, they are little commendable; but I do not see how I can avoid them and must therefore accept all their drawbacks.

I begin with one polarization that grew out of the movement itself: "liturgism." (I want to comment that this word does not stem from common use. I use it in the sense which I gave it in my previous inquiries.)

The "Liturgical Movement" came about because it had to. Under the influence of modern individualism and rationalism, the cult of the Church, heavy with mighty forms, powerful ideas, and an essential orientation toward revelation, felt itself squeezed in suppression. Religious life was limited to the subjective and the private. Consequently, the demand for something that had been pushed out began to rise up in the Church. A scientific and practical project began with the objective of renewing the liturgy in its pure form and making more room for the religious life owed to it. Obviously, a certain propensity also arises to give undue importance to the subjective. This is understandable, though, as such propensities always arise, something important is left unrecognized for a long time and is then rediscovered. A new sense of enthusiasm awakens, work and sacrifice are employed to open a discussion, but then what has been rediscovered is involuntarily overemphasized. In this case, the rediscovery of the liturgy as the Christian-Catholic core sparked a certain forgetfulness of the other forms of religious life. The monastic community and its unique environment came to be seen as the overall archetype of the Christian community. The inherent limitations of liturgical work in reality were forgotten, as were

---

3. MVG note: See Guardini, "Der Gesamtzusammenhang des christlichen Gebetslebens" [The Context of Christian Prayer Life], printed in its last edition in Alfons Kirchgässner, *Unser Gottesdienst* (Freiburg/Br., 1960), 85ff. Guardini's text appears there with the title "Piety," even though he is dealing with the discernment of much more fundamental things.

the necessities and possibilities of the liturgy, and what is most important to it. It was forgotten how religion enters the personal and communal life along with the centrality of personal experience and prayer. The individual was expected to make the liturgical forms and texts his or her own source of interior life. Something forced and exaggerated arose out of this—especially when it was paired with an aesthetic sensitivity, which was blind to the needs and tasks of daily life. This gave liturgical endeavors an unpleasant taste.

These were not the attitudes of the young people and groups who instead did the actual, responsible task. Exaggerations have a tendency to enter one's consciousness more easily than what is in the right measure. The Liturgical Movement seemed to represent an image of the religious life, but it was out of context and lacked an authentic connection to reality, triggering serious reservations. Its defenders demanded that parishes adopt Latin chant as their regular form of liturgical music. They rejected "pious devotions of the people" such as the Stations of the Cross, the Rosary, and various texts in diocesan song books; and they underestimated the great significance of the vernacular language in Church song. They did not see how everything carries a personality and peculiarity that must enter individual lives of prayer and affect them. Indeed, they failed to recognize that the personality as such is not just part of the whole but also constructs the living and exclusive *you* brought before God, and, in this way, it demands its own realm of prayer where the liturgy has only limited significance. Consequently, the situation came to be quite foreign to reality and crooked. And then—you may think—if the founders of the Liturgical Movement veered into exaggerations, how much more must these have appeared with those who took up the task and developed it further, especially those people who tend to replace dedicated work with slogans and heartfelt enthusiasm with misguided zeal.

When a good effort in itself has been made for a long time, the moment will eventually arise when it suddenly enters the consciousness of the general public. While it previously had to assert itself over obstacles, it suddenly gains contemporary importance. It is an important but also precarious moment since it carries the danger of jumping to hasty, unskilled, and incoherent action. This moment arose for the liturgical work, as it would for any other. Over the first few years, many clergymen and laypeople came to understand the importance of the movement, and now something started within it that was well-meaning, but often fatal in its effects. It had long been recognized that the crux of Church life did not lay in the work comparable with members of a certain association but in what was actually religious. People began to recognize overtly the liturgy as the lifeblood of one's religious life and began to worship accordingly.

Over time, habits of worship developed, various in kind and form, which became precious to the Christian people. The pedagogical ability of the zealous did not correspond often to the rise of reorganizational tasks and new beginnings. Furthermore, liturgical texts and customs are not such that they can easily be transferred into the circumstances of every community. At the same time, then, arose the responsibility to adapt communities to liturgical customs that the zealous were often unfit to fulfill. From all of this emerged what can be called *liturgical dilettantism*.

With the conviction that man could only pray in the language he uses in daily life, the vernacular was emphasized in the liturgy. Prayer texts were translated and spoken aloud together. As a result, the idea that liturgical ministry was carried out not only by the priest but also by the congregation began to take hold. Efforts were made to make the liturgical actions more widely understood and to include the faithful in them. The importance of the living form in spiritual and religious matters was recognized, and efforts were made to emphasize liturgical symbols more strongly. The religious power of Gregorian chant was rediscovered, and an attempt was also made to *translate* it: to adapt its melodies for the translated texts to the structure and tone of the [vernacular] language. Thus, there was a great number and variety of endeavors to create what is more or less justifiably called the *liturgy of the people* [Volksliturgie]. Much was not only well-meant, but also handled correctly. Some, though, suffered shortcomings. Very often, the latter attempts were taken out of context, became arbitrary, and enacted inconsistently, naturally giving rise to confusion. If something seemed good at the time, it was taken up in practice, but in picking and choosing in this way, necessarily connected elements were rashly torn asunder. Most of all, the attempts lacked crucial predispositions.

To translate a text well, one requires not only good philological and theological knowledge, but also a significant command of the languages. These requirements were seldom found in all those zealots; indeed, they rarely spoke any Latin, and often not even the vernacular very well. Therefore, they produced objectively and linguistically impossible texts. To accentuate the symbolic core of an action, one does not just need to have deep liturgical knowledge, but also a gift for layout and presentation. Too often, both were lacking, and the shoddy inadequacy of some celebrations, called liturgical, made the people wish the old ways had remained, for at least those carried the sacrality of tradition. The same was true when dealing with all the faithful and how to involve them in the sacred actions. This effort demanded much patience, reflection, and tactfulness; the absences of which cause confusion and indignation to grow. The task of composing a melody, which lives in the tradition of Gregorian chant and relates to the people, demands both a thorough understanding of the wonderful art of choral chant and pedagogical skill; and nobody will argue that these skills are easy to find.

Undue associations between certain liturgical motifs and specific opinions—such as an unexplained conviction about the position of the laity in the Church, the relationship between ethics and religion, and the like—were fatal. The contrast between the older and younger generations was also aggravated. Personal tensions between the priest and chaplain, or between the clergy of one congregation and those of another, became apparent, and other merely human sympathies played into these kind of matters. None of this put the correctness of the liturgical concerns into question; but it disturbed serious work, created confusion, and, in the eyes of those who did not understand what it was all about, put the whole liturgical effort into a bad light.

One can therefore understand how not only hesitations but also enmity grew against these new efforts in the liturgy, even though this enmity often lacked just basis and the necessary competence.

Opposition to liturgism in particular arose, directly from the practical demands of the present situation. The attitude it is said to express may be called "practicalism." The word is not nice, but I cannot come up with a better one.

The proponents of liturgism had forgotten that "the Sabbath is for man." While they correctly asserted that most important things for religious life are done purely for the greater glory of God, the needs of quotidian life unfortunately and detrimentally slipped their minds. By contrast, the representatives of the pole of practicalism could point to their results. They said that divine worship was meant to be edifying; therefore, it had to grow out of the predisposition of souls in a given time. It served to educate ethically; therefore, it had to orient itself to ethical effects. They argued that the only important aspects of divine worship are those that immediately effect one's practical life; therefore, any contemplative liturgy that is oriented toward the eternal is futile. And so forth.

As opposed to the out-of-touch-with-reality endeavors of liturgism, this critique was right, but not when applied to the living liturgy of the Church. It also swung the pendulum too far, slipping into the opposite extreme of what liturgism had fallen into, which is no less dangerous. "Practicalism" has developed in modernity, and its shift in meaning resulted in social, economic, and ethical problems. Its intent was to help Christians overcome new challenges. However, it shifted the center of caretaker of souls into organizational and pedagogical work, and it inquired into the sense of religious things, therefore also into the liturgy, where it sought to overcome challenges. Essentially it misconstrued the essence of religious life. It forgot that the liturgy has a dignity of its own. Since it deals with God, it has a meaning in itself and is not subordinate to any practical effect. At times this attitude reached indeed high levels, for example, when it was affirmed that the dealing with eternal things and a relation to God was purposeless and it was condemned as a "waste of time." Therefore it understood in the liturgy something obsolete and superfluous that needed to be discarded in favor of more contemporary forms of worship and more effectual methods, something that could be reduced to moral or any other meaning.

The first and most important sense of the liturgy, to give glory to God, was misunderstood. Forgotten was that it exists to let man breathe the atmosphere of the holy service and to enable him to grow into it. Chasing fast results, this approach destroyed an irreplaceable means for the care of souls. The liturgy is only sacred to the extent that it is not used for alternative purposes. It can grow into an ever burning, still light, like a constantly warm and mild glow, a silent, clarifying, and shaping power; but for this, it needs the calm and freedom of unintentional development. Practicalism ["Dumbing down"], that is, oversimplification of the liturgy overlooked all of this. Pressed by the needs of modern life, it sought rapid, often even statistically tangible, results, thereby neglecting it as one of the most fruitful, dense, and lasting means to gain a positive effect.

A third direction, which we should call *conservatism*, recognized the proper significance of the contemplative life. Conservatism understood that prayer and liturgy are meaningful not just because of their moral and structural character, but also in themselves, in relation to God, and in the service of his majesty. It took the importance of tradition into account in these things, giving due honor to all things traditional and the wisdom of ancient experience. It fought against the way in which *practicalism* subordinated prayer and liturgy to the practical aspects of the moment, as well as the hasty attempts of liturgism to divert all attempts to form the liturgy according to the liturgical demands. This digression was justified as long as it addressed the efforts of the well-intended but incompetent dilettantism, while the confusion of these experiments with the serious and responsible work of a true liturgical renewal was wrong and fateful. The dangerous tendency to discard all to which one is not *accustomed* shows itself in these errors.

Conservatists[4] understood *traditional* to include everything that was *good*, and *new* to reference everything *un-ecclesial*. Anything anyone did that differed from what had always been done, they took as a sign of a revolutionary spirit. Did they not, however, consider the truth of the liturgy? An example of this is the difficulty that naturally comes with changing a previous practice: in order to make proper and fitting changes in the liturgy, practices that had been established in the fruitless nineteenth century—they themselves built up over older and treasured pious devotions—had to be given up. Alternatively, a difficulty that naturally accompanies practices long held without change: that the repetition of prayers and devotional practices become mindless and conventional, losing their heartfelt substance and power. Age and tradition are important, but they should not render one blind if something traditional is substandard or even poor; otherwise, the question of the saintly Bishop Cyprian will come to mind: should habit have more weight than truth?

---

4. Translator's note: As Guardini notes, he "shall" invent a term for this group, which he calls "conservatists." This is a neologism created by Guardini even in German (*Konservatisten* instead of *Konservative*). His meaning is not fully comparable with the modern understanding of "conservative," since he seems rather to imply that the "conservation" of an element in the liturgy became the sole intention at the cost of explanation and proper introduction, which in turn is emphasized (potentially too strongly) by the "practicalists."

Most of all, the conservatists did not understand that liturgy in the life of the parish community ought not be held in any more esteem than is owed to it. The enemies of the liturgical renewal often and repeatedly accepted their *ecclesialist* view and were strongly opinioned in dogmatic and disciplinary topics. But is it not strange that they easily pass over the fact that the liturgy is the unequivocal ancient cult of the Church based on permanent laws? Should one not be surprised that the people who share exactly this attitude toward all things traditional cast aside the worth of most ancient and sacred Tradition in favor of the most recent devotional practices? Or when they, who are quick to argue with the *lex credendi* against every speck of opposition, are quickly ready to forget that there is also a *lex orandi*, which is not fulfilled simply by following rubrics, but rather through a truly religiously ordered life imbued with love that permeates the liturgy ever deeper? It is alarming that in the Church there is a wonderfully rich, honorable tradition that underlies an equally deep and strong frame of liturgical legislation, yet the practical thinker does not give credit where it would be due. Indeed, whosoever should bear the safeguarding of tradition often falls under suspicion by instead always introducing novel forms of devotions, . . . and may succumb to a questionable understanding of what the Church is. All too often, devotions—sometimes of questionable value—for communities or private individuals dominate and take up the religious life of the community. It is rare to find a serious and consequential introduction into the liturgy.

Actions of the highest rank are cast aside, and with them irreplaceable possibilities for the care of souls are lost.

The celebration of the Eucharist has too many times been reduced to the character of a pious devotion. The variety of the liturgical life has disappeared on a large scale, and interior monotony has taken its place, the fateful effects of which we have not even sufficiently understood. The praxis of the sacraments has been separated from their essential meaning and become alienated. Much more could be added here.

Conservatists explain that a proper introduction is too complicated and the liturgy too unfamiliar to the people—though there remains reason to doubt if they have truly attempted to lead the people further in its understanding. They say that women would not be able to understand certain elements of the liturgy and that supposedly men need powerful liturgical nourishment; but it is very doubtful which women and which men had a say in the making of this opinion. Instead of ceasing their attempts with the declaration of these hasty conclusions, they should have tried first to sharpen the men's sense for the great forms of the liturgy and awaken women's sensitivity as to foster a deeper understanding of the enriching mystery. Often the *people* understand much more than one would think. Anyone who honestly and patiently tries will make this joyous and—reflecting one's own assessment—humbling experience. Obviously one must first know what is at stake in order to do this work with conviction and true readiness.

Both groups—conservatists and practicalists—know far less of the religious needs of the faithful than one may think having heard their repetitive chatter about their own experiences. Otherwise, they would recognize that people are turned away from the Church by old or mediocre pious devotions. At the same time, they want to retain that the liturgy is simply a vital part of people's lives. Should you tell them this, they will retort arguing that the faithful are proud and allegedly always want something special and they will bring up the hubris of the young who always think they know better—a way of pushing aside uncomfortable truths and silencing another's argument that, really, is equally imbalanced and dangerous.

Sometimes the very same strict judges of aspiration to liturgical reform have themselves no real concept of what liturgy actually is. For me to point out the inadequacies of the liturgical training clergymen have lately received will count as no sterile criticism. For a long time, liturgy was one of the more neglected subjects, summarized under the term *pastoral theology* and perceived as something quite secondary in the whole of theological education. It is thus understandable if many imagine something to be there, yet do not understand its meaning. They recognize a kind of religious representation that has somewhat developed over time. They posit that one has to enact this representation, as far the rules require it, but which needs to be overcome as quickly as possible in order to move on to actually important and practically effective things. With the above-mentioned adversities in mind, it must be said that the conservatists are actually right in the struggle against liturgical efforts, because what they understand when they hear this word is indeed not the real liturgy of the Church. What the conservatists are fighting is a straw man. In the fight against this phantom, however, they overlook what is real and what is of the greatest importance for the pastoral care that is important to them.

In the foregoing, my dear and honorable friend, I have tried to draw out four points upon which the liturgical question rests. I hope I have not been one-sided, but that I properly showed the difficulty of the situation. I hope it is evident that I appreciate the concerns of the responsible persons. Allow me, however, to express another relevant concern: the danger of a short circuit that Church officials can run into.

Ecclesiastical authorities are responsible for the order of religious life; they are justified in being suspicious of arbitrariness and inadequate discipline, of all that lacks and that rings of artificiality. Now, this may raise the concern that they may want to create *order at all costs* and thereby bring valuable [reformative] efforts to a standstill. I already said that I have been involved in liturgical work for almost thirty-five years, so I think I have an idea about how important the things are with which we are dealing. I personally know many of those who are trying to help; some of them are dear friends of many years. I know how much love and work they put into their efforts and that their efforts root in a loyalty to the Church. These persons should not be met with any more or less doubt than anyone else. Some things simply cannot be done at certain times—it is all the more important that what we do now be done in the right way. This being said, based on the trust that you have placed in me, I solemnly and seriously request that you help ensure that the danger just described does not become a reality.

It goes without saying that the ecclesiastical authorities intervene against arbitrary innovations that are neither justified by office nor by capabilities. It is more than justified that they demand restraint from their clergy, especially the younger ones. However, on the same token, a lot depends on the fact that they do not withdraw their trust from those who have been working seriously and responsibly in these matters for a long time and that they protect them from attacks against their attitude and work.

What liturgical work needs is time. Much has to be done, and the tasks are difficult. A lot of theoretical knowledge, a lot of practical experience, and manifold skills (linguistic and musical in kind) are necessary to proceed. Those working on liturgical matters ask for patience. A lot hangs still in the balance, which must be discerned; this is necessary for something good to arise.

Recently, there have been attacks on liturgical work that have met with a strong response. Certainly, they stem from real concern for the Church, and my own account has shown that there was reason to do so; but I fear that they have not always worked for the better. Above all, they do not see the liturgy for what it is. Fruitful criticism should be born out of a genuine, great, and heartfelt image of the liturgy; here, that is not the case. The liturgy is well recognized and praised, and its care is advocated—but in the end, the restrictions and concerns that arise out of zealous work give the liturgical renewal a suspect appearance, and to many it seems best that everything stay the same. But as far as criticism is concerned, it is not uncommon for it to work with a method that everyone is accustomed to. Factual procedures must be taken into consideration. Individual cases that rightly deserve criticism are eagerly collected; but sadly, there is a great lack of justice, and those who point fingers neither understand the motives behind the abuses nor appreciate the resistance with which reformers have to struggle. Instead, mistakes are immediately interpreted in the most damning way and presented as the products of subjective, arbitrary, ecclesiastical dispositions.

It is particularly unjust how everything careless, foolish, exaggerated, and skewed on the part of liturgical work is gathered, but the mistakes of the earlier methods are overlooked. If one were to sift through the literature and practices of old congregations, associations, missions, retreat and pilgrimage systems, etc., one could easily compile an arbitrarily long list of things that would be at least as bad as what is criticized now—*at least* just as bad because these span a much longer period of time and experience, and therefore had a much greater possibility of rectification.

Criticism is good, but it must be just and objective, otherwise it does not edify but destroy. Errors are unfortunate, but errors exist everywhere, and what are at stake are the motives that form the basis of these errors. Where have good thoughts not already been misused? What would the critics say if you showed them all things vulnerable for attacks that are found in literature and practice against which they argue? You would be outraged. They would ask for their thoughts to be seen as what they really are. They would say that your argument is weak, because you took the position with a weak and irrelevant core. If you want to debate, then you should do it honestly—that is, facing the essence of your adversary's position.

Critics of a renewal would be right in making this demand; but they may get satisfaction that they act this way! I know enough of theory and practice that my response should not be overlooked, but I will only retort if what is under attack—which is the business of the Church herself—requires it. Rather, I turn to you with confidence and with you to our bishops, convinced that they will distinguish truth from error, the essential from the unimportant, the permanent from the passing, and will not yield that an easily flammable mood honors something that has endured many years and is supported by deep love for the Church.

My presentation has been imperfect and deficient. None of the diverse currents of thought that I have mentioned will agree with it. Everyone will say that the truth has not shined forth from these pages and instead that criticism has been too heavy. However, to avoid that, you would have to write a book. The most fundamental problems would not have to be developed; they already stand in full force. Perhaps you will ask what ought to happen on a practical level? I must omit an answer here and direct you to works which have already been written or which are in preparation. My intention here was only to explain some currents that are at work in our contemporary situation and to point out to whom they relate within the ecclesiastical life. Should it be fitting to summarize with a conclusion, I would want to do so in the following way: the liturgical life has always been important to the Church and will always remain so. Therefore, it demands thoughtful care and unfolding. With dedication and tireless patience, the pastor must introduce his faithful to the liturgy. He can only do so when he himself has reached its essence. To do that, he must conserve the liturgy in its theological prefiguration and its continuation in the area reserved for it. He must understand that the liturgy is no less important in its theoretical and practical aspects than dogmatics and ethics.

The parish model of the liturgy must not be based on the monastery or cathedral churches—which, of course, are very important in their own place—but must be determined from the real needs and possibilities of the parish.

This must be guided by subjective discretion and at will, but only according to the *lex orandi* of the Church. At the same time, it must employ the real freedom of creation and design wherever this law of the Church allows. What this means in detail still requires careful clarification. People must be found who have the necessary prerequisites.

The liturgy is important. Personal religious life is also important and indispensable. It is connected with but does not coincide with the liturgical; they stand apart in a lively and fruitful tension. Therefore, liturgical education must run parallel with personal prayer, contemplation, the use of Holy Scripture, a religious understanding of everyday life, and a religious interpretation of existence in general.

Between personal religious life and liturgical prayer stands *folkloric devotion*, a real and separate aspect that finds particular expression in our hymnbooks. It receives important rules, suggestions, and powers that derive from both sides, yet it is rooted in its own laws.

This area must be given special and dedicated care, and I believe that there is a lot to be done here. Deteriorated texts must be restored; ancient treasures must be unearthed. And the truly gifted will experience a beautiful taste of creating new elements.

German church hymns warrant special attention. Their current state is altogether unpleasant. The most beautiful songs are sung least. It is safe to say that these days the more often a song is sung, the shallower is its text and the more sentimental is its melody. The good melodies are fragmented and often in bad condition in themselves; and the way in which they are sung is most often all but lively. Neglected ancient treasures must be uncovered, and new songs should be written—but obviously only by those who are truly equipped for it.

This letter is already saturated, and will hold no more. Therefore I want to ensure you, most reverend friend, that I have been ardently attentive to lay out these thoughts with as much dedication to the truth and awe of the Churchly authority which I can witness in your presence.

In trust that you will feel the same way, I ask you to accept the expression of my most humble loyalty.

— **Romano Guardini**